Simple Serger Sewing

Edited by Julie Johnson

HOUSE of
WHITE
BIRCHES
PUBLISHERS
SINCE 1947

Simple Serger Sewing

Editor Julie Johnson

Art Director Brad Snow

Publishing Services Director Brenda Gallmeyer

Managing Editor Dianne Schmidt

Assistant Art Director Nick Pierce

Copy Supervisor Michelle Beck

Copy Editor Amanda Ladig

Technical Editors Angeline Buckles, Marla Laux

Graphic Arts Supervisor Ronda Bechinski

Graphic Artists Glenda Chamberlain, Edith Teegarden

Production Assistants Marj Morgan, Judy Neuenschwander

Technical Artist Nicole Gage

Photography Supervisor Tammy Christian

Photography Matthew Owen

Photo Stylist Tammy Steiner

Printed in China
First Printing: 2009
Library of Congress Control Number: 2008936679
Hardcover ISBN: 978-1-59217-246-7

DRGbooks.com

1 2 3 4 5 6 7 8 9

Love at First Stitch

I love to fall in love, especially with my serger. Yes, I'll admit it. I've had this love affair going on for a long, long time and every time I serge, I fall in love all over again.

Why do I fall in love every time I use my serger? A serger is fast; it sews about 1500 stitches per minute. Not only is it fast, but it cuts as it sews leaving a beautifully finished edge. Set your serger for a 4-thread overlock and you can seam, trim and edge finish in one step. So not only is the stitching fast and professional, but you eliminate steps by using just one machine.

In a nutshell, using a serger allows you to have professional crafted projects completed quickly and easily—leaving you more time to do what you really love—sewing with your serger!

"So what's the catch," is what you're probably asking. The catch is that you need to get to know your serger. That's what this book is all about, getting to know your serger simply and easily. Included in the book are some easy-to-follow reference materials on serger basics and some guidance on serger sewing. What makes this book extra special is that you learn as you serge home decor, gifts and wearables.

I love my serger. But, I know that when you're done serging the projects in this book, you'll fall in love with your serger too.

Here's to falling in love, again and again.

Until next time.

Julie

Julie Johnson, Editor

Contents

Getting to Know Your Serger

How a Serger Sews 7

Types of Serger Stitches 10

All About Thread 12

Setting Your Tension 14

Turning Corners, Curves & Openings 16

Serging Seams & Hems 18

Serge Sweet Baby

Funsie Onesie 21

Summer Breeze 24

Yo-yo Baby Quilt 27

Heirloom Baby Bib 30

Quick Cuddly Quilt 34

Baby Steps 38

Bow Tie for Baby 41

Cozy Cover 44

Sergable Wearables

Smart Serged Sweatshirt 49
All-Stitched-Up Denim 54
Rolled Around Tee 58
Trim a Tee 61
Pintuck Shirt 64
Rectangle to Jacket 66
Puzzle Blouse 69
Tailored for Me Oxford 72
Serge Simple Shirt 76
Princess P.J.s 79
Fast & Breezy Skirt 84
Flatlock Fleece 86
Coverstitch: More Than Hems 90
Serge a Simple Jacket 94
Jeweled Batik Jacket 98

Around the House

Button Valance 102
Fly-Away Drapery 105
Jelly Roll Valance 108
Quick & Easy Pillow Cover 111
Picture-Perfect Place Setting 114
Reversible Batik Topper 118
Scrappy Braid Place Mat 122
Elegant Embroidered Runner 125
Heirloom Pillow 128
Polka Dot Tuffet 131

More Than a Gift

Tote Trio 136
Rolled-Around Tree Skirt 140
Woven Candle Mat 143
Serge Organize 146
Cupcake Apron 150
Sweet Tote 153
Flatlock Patchwork Tote 156
Serger Bag Trio 160
Beach Bag 164
Jelly Roll Shopping Tote 167
Starry Night Tote 170

Special Thanks 175
Sewing Sources 176
Basic Sewing Supplies & Equipment 176

Getting to Know Your Serger

By learning these serger shortcuts, you'll be able to save time on your sewn projects and have professional looking end results. Sewing just can't get any better!

How a Serger Sews A serger is simple to understand, once you know the differences between a sewing machine and a serger.

Serger Sewing

All sergers, regardless of the number of threads, needles or electronic enhancements, work in the same simple-to-understand way. Instead of sewing stitches with a conventional bobbin system, sergers "serge" stitches with a looper system.

Similar to a sewing machine, sergers have adjustable stitch length and width, and adjustable presser foot tensions. Unlike a sewing machine, sergers have a cutting system and today, most sergers have a differential feed system (Figure 1).

A) Chain Stitch Looper (Part of the Lower Looper System)
B) Feed Dogs
C) Fly Wheel
D) Lower Knife
E) Lower Looper
F) Lower Looper Tensions
G) Needles
H) Needle Thread Tensions
I) Presser Foot
J) Spool Holders for Thread
K) Thread Guide
L) Upper Looper Tension
M) Upper Knife
N) Upper Looper

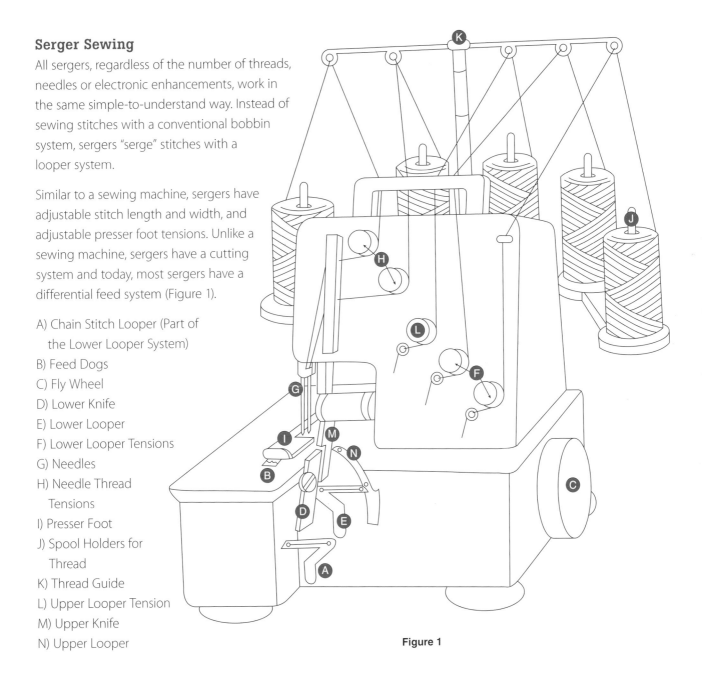

Figure 1

Serger Stitch Formation

The looper system and one or more needles form the serger stitches. The looper system "loops" or throws threads around the stitch finger on the throat plate (Figure 2). As the fabric is serged, one thread loop lays on top of the fabric while the other thread loop rests underneath the fabric. The needle(s) thread catches and secures the thread loop on top of the fabric.

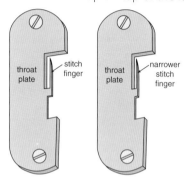

Figure 2

Care & Cleaning of Your Serger

Scheduled care and cleaning will extend the life of your serger.

Oil your machine according to your owner's manual. Most sergers require oil after eight to ten hours of use.

Clean your serger after every use by opening the front cover and removing all fabric and thread clippings. Try using your vacuum nozzle (be careful you don't suck the thread out of the loopers) or a small paint brush to brush away fabric clippings. My favorite tool for hard to reach nooks and crannies is a clean mascara brush. It's small, durable and picks up thread clippings easily. And it's cheap and readily available.

Cover your serger when not in use. This keeps dust from attaching to the blades and other internal mechanisms ensuring a longer life.

Refer to your owner's manual for more detail.

As the needle(s) thread goes through the fabric, the thread catches and secures the loop on the bottom.

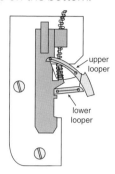

Figure 3

Most sergers have two loopers that throw the thread loops. Each looper is named by its action: the upper looper goes over the top of the stitch finger and lays thread on top of the fabric, while the lower looper passes under the stitch finger laying thread on the underside of the fabric (Figure 3).

Adjusting Stitch Length and Width

Similar to your sewing machine, the serger stitch can be widened or narrowed and lengthened or shortened. Stitch width is adjusted by changing the needle position (on some models) or by moving the stitch fingers closer or further apart on the throat plate. Stitch length is easy to adjust; simply adjust the feed dogs as one does on a conventional sewing machine.

In addition to adjusting stitch width and length, the looper and needle combination can be changed to create different stitches.

Differential Feed and Presser Foot Adjustment

Today, most sergers come with differential feed system. A differential feed system feeds the fabric

Tips & Techniques

Sometimes adjusting the stitch width or length is all that's needed for perfect tension. As a general rule, just like on your sewing machine, bulky fabric such as polar fleece or fake fur serges best with a longer stitch width and length, while sheer fabric seams look better with a narrow width and length.

"unevenly" as it is feed under the presser foot. The uneven feeding eliminates puckering, gathering or distortion (shrinking or growing) of the fabric as it's serged. The system works by moving the split feed dogs at a different rate as you serge.

Tips & Techniques

For professionally finished seams, press the seam and allowances flat to set the stitches in the seam. Lay the garment with wrong side up, and press the seam allowance open. To finish, turn the garment to the right side, and press once again.

If your serger does not have a differential feed system, you can compensate for fabric weight and stretch by adjusting the pressure of the presser foot. A lighter pressure will allow heavier and stretchy fabric to pass between the feed dogs and foot easily leaving a smoother seam. Refer to your owner's manual for more details.

Serger Cutting System

As mentioned before, one of the time saving features of a serger is the cutting system. This system works by having two blades that trim the fabric as you sew.

What you need to know about the cutting system is that on most sergers, the upper blade can be moved out of the way. This is important for cover stitch and some flatlock applications.

Finally, because of how the cutting system works, most often it's the lower blade that dulls and needs to be replaced. §

Tips & Techniques

Always test a swatch of fabric to determine whether the fabric is rippling prior to sewing the actual project. Often, loosening the pressure adjustment for the serger is enough for the fabric to lay flat when sewn.

Cutting Techniques & Tricks

Dull blades will not leave a clean cut edge. Man-made fabrics, like polyester and tricot, cause your blades to dull more quickly than natural fibers. To extend the life of your blades, use the cutting system for just trimming stray threads, not for cutting. If you're planning on serging the seams from ⅝ inch to ⅜ inch, trim the seams from the pattern prior to or as you cut the pattern from the fabric.

Try this trick for lengthening the life of your blades. After every use, clean each blade with rubbing alcohol. Then, lightly apply a coat of sewing machine oil to each blade. The rubbing alcohol will remove residue and the sewing machine oil will reduce friction ensuring sharper longer lasting serger blades.

To ensure a smooth cut on bulky fabric from your serger, simply clip about an inch into your fabric with your sheers. This will help the feed dogs and presser foot grab your fabric leaving a straight seam at entry.

Finally, never serge over pins. Though the pin will be neatly chopped in two, cutting the pin will nick your lower blade and leave a dull mark. Instead of pins, try using a fabric glue stick instead.

Types of Serger Stitches There are five basic serger stitches. These stitches, in general, can have a wide or narrow seam width and a long or short stitch length. All are capable of using decorative thread.

3- or 4-Thread Overlock Stitch

This is the greatest stitch on the serger and is what the serger was designed to do–provide a simple, fast way to sew and edge finish seams. This stitch is formed by using one or two needles and both loopers (Figure 1).

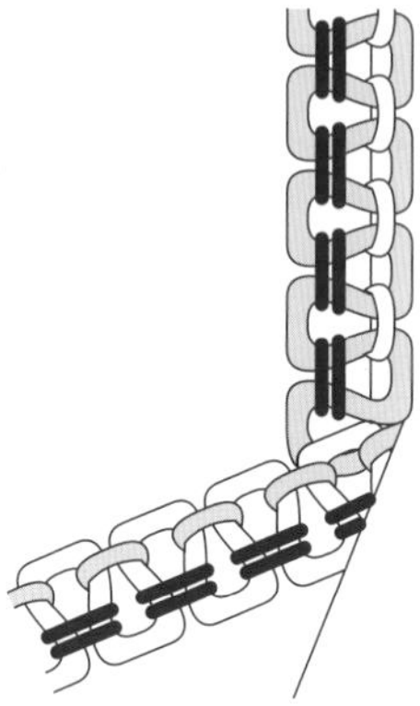

Available on most sergers as an optional 3-thread or 4-thread overlock (overedge or merrow stitch), it's strong and durable. It's perfect for swimwear and knits because of the way the stitch is constructed. It has both strength and stretch.

Figure 1

Most wovens are fine with an overlock stitch, unless the seam is weight bearing, such as a shoulder seam. For reinforcement on weight-bearing seams, serge over twill tape. To get started, lay the twill underneath the needle(s) on the serger and under the pressure foot. Serge into place.

Chain Stitch

Sewn with the "backward" shaped looper and the outside needle, this stitch is most often associated with ready-to-wear. A chain stitch is very easy to pull out by grabbing one thread and the whole seam will unravel (Figure 2).

Most sergers will sew the chain stitch with either a 2- or 3-thread stitch as the edge finish. When sewn, it looks like a traditional seam—perfect for wovens.

With the flexibility of today's sergers, you can use this stitch as for beautiful textural effects.

Figure 2

Flat Lock & Ladder Stitch

This is a 2- or 3-thread stitch made by using one needle and for a 2-thread flat lock, the upper looper only, for a 3-thread flat lock, both loopers (Figure 3). The needle tension is adjusted (loosened) so the needle thread is pulled across the underneath side of the fabric to the outside edge with the upper looper tension set for traditional edge finishing.

Figure 3

On some sergers, you'll have a small hook that fits into one of the loopers (Figure 4 on page 11). Refer to your owner's manual for set-up.

Try a flat lock stitch using decorative thread or yarn in the upper looper for a decorative effect. Loosen the looper tension(s) for a decorative thread or yarn covers the top of the fabric. After the seam is complete, gently pull on the seam to open and lay the fabric flat displaying the decorative thread.

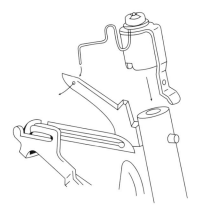

Figure 4

The ladder stitch is the "wrong" side of the flat lock stitch. This stitch has become very popular for heirloom serging. The ladder stitch is used for delicate lace insertion and serging over satin ribbon.

A variation on the ladder stitch is called Fagoting (Figure 5). Often used in heirloom sewing, this is a ladder stitch catching only the edges of the fabric.

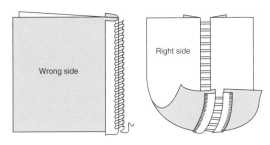

Figure 5

When using either the ladder stitch or the fagoting, make sure that you place the fabric with right sides together (for a flat lock stitch, the fabric is positioned with wrong sides together).

Cover Stitch

The cover stitch is a relatively new serger stitch. It's made by using 2- or 3-needles and the lower looper (Figure 6a and b). The cutting system is disengaged for the cover stitch.

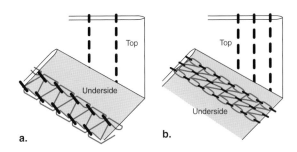

Figure 6

The cover stitch started its life as the perfect stitch for hemming knits because it has the most stretch of the serger stitches. However, you'll see this stitch used for more than hemming. Often the underside is used as a decorative stitch to make cover stitch lace.

Rolled Edge

The rolled edge is a simple decorative stitch formed with one needle and both loopers (Figure 7). The tension for the lower looper thread is tightened to pull the upper looper thread around the raw edge of the fabric as the fabric. Typically the rolled edge uses a narrow stitch finger on the throat plate.

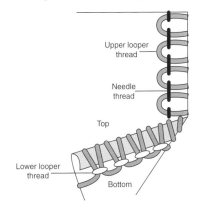

Figure 7

You'll see this stitch used for napkin edges, slightly pulled on knit fabrics as a lettuce edge trim or as a simple edge finish replacing the conventional sewing machine narrow edge.

Another application of the rolled edge is to roll over a medium weight of fishing line. This is a perfect edge finish for chiffon or lace and gives a soft lift to the fabric. §

All About Thread Threading your serger is really simple once you know how. It's like riding a bike, once you learn how, you'll never forget!

Threading Your Serger

The easiest way to thread your serger is to never unthread it. When you need to change the threads, clip the threads and tie a square knot with the "old" and "new" thread. Make sure the knot is secure. Loosen the tension to zero (no tension) on all needles and loopers, and pull the thread through the guides. Be sure to watch the knot as it goes through the tension dial (I've had many a knots come undone at this point) and also as you pull it through the eye of the needles.

When it is necessary to rethread your serger, it's recommended to thread the serger in this order:

      Lower looper
      Upper looper
      Inner needle
      Outer needle

Tips & Techniques

Invest in a looper threader. This is a great tool that will help should your lower looper ever unthread. As an alternative pick up dental picks from the drug store. These are light weight, flexible and have a loop at the end for grabbing the thread and pulling it through the narrow opening on the lower looper.

Thread Choice

Thread choice is important for a serger. Use the same brand of thread in all needles and loopers for a balanced stitch and easier tension adjustments. Invest in a quality thread because this thread will have a smooth uniform consistency.

Invest in cone thread in your basic sewing colors. I keep on hand cones of black, white, off-white, gray and brown thread. Cones are designed for the thread to unwind from the cone without spinning. As such, cone thread typically has a smoother finish, is wrapped or twisted tighter and is finer than most brands of spool thread. In other words, it's designed for serger sewing.

As an alternative to cone thread, wind bobbins from your sewing spools. The needle thread, if any, is the thread that will be seen from the outside of the garment, so try to match this thread if possible. Because it uses less thread than the loopers, invest in a small spool or wind several bobbins.

Other thread choices are available for decorative stitching. These include:

Woolly nylon: used for lingerie sewing or for the rolled edge, this is a thread that has little or no twist. Because of the small amount of twist, it provides exceptional seam coverage. Best when used in either the upper or lower looper, though I have used it in the needle when I sew lingerie. Caution, don't put woolly nylon thread in the dryer as it will melt.

Rolled edge with woolly nylon.

Metallic thread: used for its decorative appeal, this thread has little or no stretch. Though it does make a beautiful rolled edge, because it has little or no stretch, this should not be the thread choice for your first rolled edge. Try using it in the flat lock or overedge stitch only in one or both loopers.

Flatlock with metallic thread.

Baby or fine yarn, pearl cotton: used for decorative effects, these fine yarns in the overlock stitch can be used in place of binding on polar fleece jackets and blankets. Use the yarn in either the upper looper for the overedge stitch, or in the upper looper for a flat lock stitch or for a heavier rolled edge.

Flatlock with pearl cotton.

Securing Thread Tails

A great advantage of having a serger is that you never, well hardly ever, worry about jamming the serger by not sewing on fabric. Believe me, in my 28 years of serger sewing, I've done just about everything.

The only problem with the serger is how to secure the beginning and ending thread to keep it from dangling. For securing thread at the beginning of the seam, try:

• Serging about ½ inch onto the fabric. Raise the pressure foot and slip the thread tail under the needles to catch the tail in the serging.

• Using large needle slipping the thread tail into the serged seam after the seam is complete.

• Cutting the thread tails next to the fabric and applying a small drop of seam sealant. Be careful with this one; on a delicate fabric the seam sealant may show through and on certain seams (neckline), it may cause skin irritation when worn.

For securing thread at the end of the seam, try using bullets two and three. Or stitch one stitch off of the fabric. Gently pull on the needle(s) thread. Slip fabric off of the stitch finger(s). Flip fabric over. Serge about 1 inch, then serge off the fabric at an angle. Clip and use seam sealant if desired. §

Tips & Techniques

Avoid cotton thread for knits, especially swimwear because 100 percent cotton thread has very little stretch. Instead, use a high quality polyester thread on knits.

Setting Your Tension It's important to understand how to adjust your tension for professional-looking seams. Once you understand how the stitch is formed by the thread's interaction, you'll be setting your tension in no time.

Tension Rules

Most sergers have numbered tension dials making tension adjustment relatively easy. Similar to your sewing machine, tension is adjusted for different weights of fabric. As a general rule:

The more loft or thickness of the fabric, the looser the tension should be for needles and loopers. Fine or sheer fabrics need a tighter tension in both needles and loopers.

For an over-edge or standard serger stitch, a balanced serger tension occurs when the needle thread is almost buried in the fabric and the upper looper's tension allows the thread to form a "S" shape along the top fabric edge with the stitches resting on the cut edge of the fabric. The bottom tension is balanced when the lower looper forms a "V" for three thread or a "Y" for four thread over-edge stitching with the forks of the letter aligned along the cut edge of the fabric.

One more rule you may find helpful: Righty-tighty, lefty-loosey.

Applying the Rules for Looper Tension

Translated, righty-tighty, lefty-loosey means that if your upper looper thread looks like this:

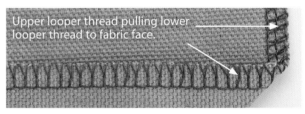

Upper looper thread pulling lower looper thread to fabric face.

or if your lower looper thread looks like this:

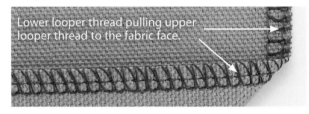

Lower looper thread pulling upper looper thread to the fabric face.

the looper tension is too tight. Turn the corresponding tension dial to the left to loosen the looper tension.

However, if your upper looper looks like this:

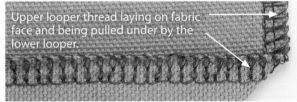

Upper looper thread laying on fabric face and being pulled under by the lower looper.

or if your lower looper thread looks like this:

Lower looper thread laying on fabric back and being pulled to fabric face by upper looper thread.

the looper tension is too loose. Turn the corresponding tension dial to the right to tighten the looper tension.

Applying the Rule for Needle Tension

The same rule applies to your inner and outer needle. For your outer needle, if the thread and the fabric looks like this:

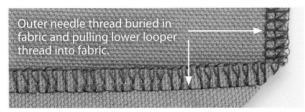

Outer needle thread buried in fabric and pulling lower looper thread into fabric.

or if your inner needle thread looks like this:

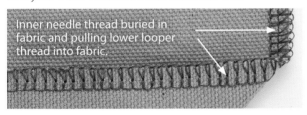

Inner needle thread buried in fabric and pulling lower looper thread into fabric.

the needle tension is too tight. Turn the corresponding tension dial to the left to loosen the needle tension.

However, if your outer needle thread looks like this:

Outer needle thread laying on top of fabric and leaving loops on fabric back.

or if your inner needle thread looks like this:

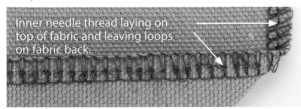

Inner needle thread laying on top of fabric and leaving loops on fabric back.

the needle(s) tension is too loose. Turn the corresponding tension dial to the right to tighten the needle tension.

Pulling it all Together

Here's what you really want to know about how to make adjusting the tension work. Again, a simple rule to follow:

Set your needle tension first, followed by setting the looper tension.

The reason for setting the needle tension first is that the stitch formation is a combination of threads looped together. If one thread is too tight or loose, another thread can compensate for that tightness or looseness. Thus, for the best-looking seams available always adjust the outside needle tension first because the outside needle thread does the brunt of the work.

If you set this tension first, followed by the inside needle tension, you'll have the strongest seam available from your serger. Once set, follow the illustrations above, and the looper tensions are easy to adjust by looking at their placement along the outside edge of the fabric. §

Tips & Techniques

When adjusting the seam tension, always start with the outside needle. If the seam is still loose, adjust both looper tensions. Remember, the serger stitch is formed due to the interlocking of the threads. If one thread is too loose, it can throw all of the thread tensions off.

Don't forget about using the rolled edge as a hem finish, especially for curved seams. Try stretching a ribbing as it's rolled to create a lettuce edge. This is a beautiful finish for child's socks or booties. By rolling over a medium weight of fishing line, you can achieve a soft ruffled effect.

Turning Corners, Curves & Openings
Because the cutting system trims the fabric before its sewn, serging shapes takes some know-how. Try a sample until you feel comfortable with the following techniques.

Corners

For an outside corner, serge one stitch past the corner, raise the pressure foot and gently pull on the needle(s) thread below the tension dial. This gives the thread enough leeway to allow the stitches to slip off of the stitch finger on the throat plate. Next, turn the fabric. Reposition the fabric under the pressure foot. Lower the pressure foot, and pull on the needle(s) thread above the tension dial to tighten the loose threads. Continue serging.

For an inside corner, serge almost to the corner (Figure 1), and fold the fabric as shown (Figure 2).

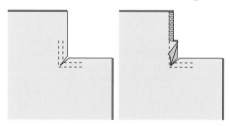

Figure 1

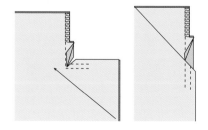

Figure 2

Serge over the inside corner and release the fabric. An alternative method is to make a small clip in the inside corner. As you serge, gently pull the fabric flat as shown.

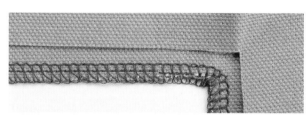

Tips & Techniques

Before you start serging, remember to use your cutting system as the guide—not the needle as you do with your conventional sewing. The serger's feed dogs begin at the cutting system. The feed dogs are longer and have substantial grip compared to your conventional sewing machine so they automatically grab and guide the fabric through the serging process.

Curves

Inside curves, such as necklines, are simple to sew. Gently pull on the fabric to make it straight (Figure 3). You'll be surprised at how much easier this is on a serger than on a conventional sewing machine.

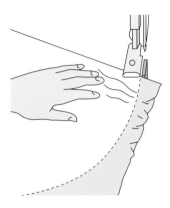

Figure 3

Outside curves require a little more fabric handling. For an outside curve, use your finger tips to continually push the fabric against the cutting system (Figure 4). Because of the feed dogs' ability to grab and evenly feed the fabric, the outside curve will turn out nicely with this technique.

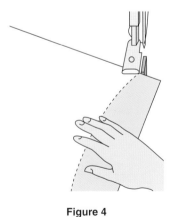

Figure 4

Tips & Techniques

To save time, only serge the sides of the pattern where the seam will be exposed as you'll grade the seam allowance to ⅛ or ¼ inch to reduce bulk.

Tips & Techniques

Easing a Curved Hem: *This hems works well for when you have a circular edge that needs a narrow hem. Set your serger for a 4-thread overlock. Simply tighten the inside needle thread, and the seam will automatically start to pucker and tighten. By adjusting the needle tension, you'll be able to slightly ease the outside edge of the fabric for seaming.*

An alternative method is to use a 3-thread overlock. Loosen the needle tension, then pull on the thread to tighten and ease the hem as needed.

Openings

For plackets, or other straight openings in the fabric, clip the fabric to the desired length (Figure 5). Pull the fabric and fold it upon itself to make it straight (Figure 6).

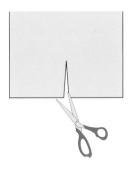

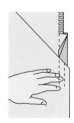

Figure 6

Figure 5

Angle toward the raw edge of the fabric as you approach the end of the placket. Slowly release the fabric as sew the point (Figure 7).

After the point is sewn, angle back so the serger is completely on the fabric. **§**

Figure 7

Serging Seams & Hems Combine your serger and sewing machine stitches to create professional looking seams for different fabric weights and weave.

Serging Seams

Traditional Seam with 3 or 4-Thread Overcasting

This seam is great for heavy fabric that needs a full seam allowance due to weave or wear. I prefer this seam when sewing tailored jackets, especially when I want to avoid time-consuming lining.

After you have cut out your pattern, use a 3- or 4-thread overlock to serge the raw edges of each pattern piece. Place each piece in front of the presser foot with the face up and serge the piece in one continuous seam. To save time, serge a few inches off each piece, then slide the next piece in front of the presser foot. Continue serging and adding pieces until all sides of all pattern pieces are complete.

Using your sewing machine, straight stitch seams, and press open (Figure 1). If you've serged the pieces all on the right side, after the seams are pressed open, the serger stitching will be consistent inside the garment.

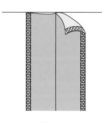

Figure 1   **Figure 2**

To avoid lining a jacket, fuse the wrong side of the jacket with fusible knit interfacing before serging. The knit interfacing is smooth on the outside allowing the jacket to easily slide on and off. For a decorative look,

try topstitching the seam allowance to the garment body on jackets with simple lines (Figure 2).

Serger Welt Seam

This seam works well with heavier fabrics where you don't want the seam exposed or want to eliminate bulk. Like the traditional seam, it's a combination of straight stitch with your sewing machine and your serger.

With wrong sides together, straight stitch the seam first. Trim one seam allowance to ¼ inch. With the wrong side of the remaining seam allowance, use a 3- or 4-thread overlock to serge the outside edge without trimming. Press the seam open, then press the serged seam over the trimmed seam. Topstitch into place (Figure 3).

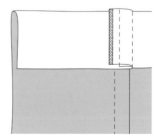

Figure 3

Traditional Overlock Seam

For some woven garments, I prefer a narrower seam allowance with a straight stitch on my machine. After the pattern is cut out, straight stitch seams and press the seam allowances flat. Using a 3- or 4-thread overlock, serge the seam allowance together, trimming allowance to ¼-inch wide (Figure 4). Repress the seam to the back of the garment or with gravity.

Figure 4

The stitch looks like ready-to-wear, so if seams are exposed, the garment will have a professional look. Some sergers will chain stitch and overcast with either a 2- or 3-thread edge finish, so you'll achieve the same look with one pass. Refer to your owner's manual for more information.

This seam is a perfect for loosely woven fabrics where it's difficult to get a tight needle tension when you one-pass serge. I also use it on weight bearing seams on some garments, when I one-pass sew the sides.

One Pass Sewing Seam

Most of my garments are sewn with a one pass seam due to the speed and ease of serging. Before you do serge the seams, make the following adjustments.

First, make sure the pattern will fit. With this type of seam, you'll have a ¼-inch seam allowance remaining (Figure 5). To extend the life of your cutting system, trim the seams from the pattern prior to cutting.

Figure 5

To determine if this is a seam choice, sample serge using a 4-thread overlock two pieces of fabric together. Open the sample fabric seam and gently pull on from the ends of the stitching. If the stitching shows, the tension needs to be tighter. If the fabric is rippling, the tension needs to be looser.

Use this seam on blouse weight fabrics, fat quarters and for quilting. It's also a great seam for knits, especially a T-shirt weight, swimwear and dancewear.

French Serger Seam

This is a great seam for sheer fabric. Set your serger to a mid-width 3-thread overlock. With wrong sides together, serge and trim seam allowance. Press serged seam flat to set stitches. Open the seam and press the

serging to one side. Fold the fabric right sides together and straight stitch just past the serged seam encased in the fabric (Figure 6).

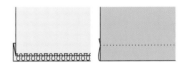

Figure 6

This seam works well for side seams, sheer draperies and for when you don't want the serging to show.

Serging Hems
Blind Hem

Set your serger for a 3- or 4-thread overlock. Determine the hem depth. Lightly press with wrong sides together. With the wrong side of the fabric facing up, fold the hem almost in half with the raw edge under the original fold. Serge into place, barely catching the folded fabric edge (Figure 7).

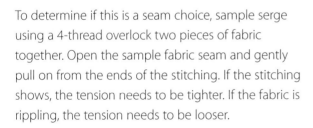

Figure 7

Use this hem as a finish for heavier fabrics, such as wool or denim. It also is a fast finish for draperies, too. With practice, you'll be able to make this hem unseen.

Mock Band

Set your serger for a 3- or 4-thread overlock. This is perfect hem for lightweight woven or knit tops or pants. The band is folded the same as for the blind hem; the difference is that you trim this edge off and take a deeper bit of the fabric (Figure 8).

Figure 8

Think outside the box (or band) for this one. Use accent colors for trimming, or run elastic through the opening for an elastic casing. Another variation for this hem finish is to sandwich a piece of lace or rickrack within the fold. §

Serge Sweet Baby

Making a timely gift for a special arrival can be a challenge for today's woman on the go. Try these simple-to-serge projects for on-time delivery.

Funsie Onesie

Transform an ordinary onesie into a delightfully sweet outfit. Add on some coordinating socks and your little one is baby-boutique chic!

By Lorine Mason

Finished size
Infant's 3–6 months

Materials
• Purchased long-sleeve onesie
• Purchased infant socks
• 44/45-inch lightweight woven fabric:
    ¼ yard floral print
    ⅛ yard coordinating print
• Threads:
    2 cones woolly nylon
    3 or 4 cones polyester or poly/cotton blend
• 5 matching buttons
• Gathering foot for the serger
• Basic sewing supplies and equipment

Cutting
From floral print fabric:
• Cut a 5-inch strip the width of the fabric for skirt.

From coordinating print fabric:
• Cut one 1½-inch bias strip (Figure 1).

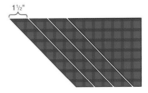

Figure 1

Assembly
Use a 3- or 4-thread overlock with a ¼-inch wide seam and medium stitch length unless otherwise stated, with woolly nylon in upper and lower looper to add softness and stretch. Use polyester or poly/cotton thread in needles for strength. Use a low heat setting when pressing or drying to avoid melting the woolly nylon.

1. Center onesie on cutting mat. Using ruler and rotary cutter, measure 2½ inches down from underarm seams and cut onesie in half (Figure 2). Measure circumference of cut edge and add 1 inch. Set aside, being careful not to stretch.

2½"

Figure 2

2. Trim bias strip to the above measurement. Serge short ends of strip together on the diagonal (Figure 3).

Figure 3

3. With right sides together, serge the edge of the bias strip to the raw edge of the onesie top.

4. Fold skirt strip in half, matching ends. Mark ½ inch from top edge and 7 inches from end. Draw a curved line connecting the two marks. Cut on curved line (Figure 4).

Fold

½"

7"

Figure 4

Tips & Techniques

Place a large dinner plate upside down between the marks and trace the plate edge to obtain an even curve.

5. Adjust serger for a rolled hem, and finish hem along bottom (curved) edge of skirt.

6. Use gathering foot to gather the top edge of the skirt, or use sewing machine to sew two rows of gathering stitches ⅛ inch apart, then pull threads to gather.

7. With right sides together, pin skirt to bottom edge of bias strip, overlapping points of curved ends slightly off onesie center front. Distribute gathers evenly by gently pulling on gathering threads.

8. With wrong side of skirt facing right side of onesie bottom, serge together. Press seams toward bias strip.

9. Evenly space and securely sew buttons to bias strip.

10. Using a rolled edge, serge the top edge of each sock stretching as you sew to create a ruffled lettuce edge. Securely sew a button to the toe of each sock. §

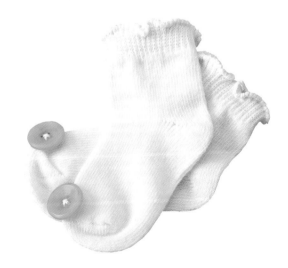

Summer Breeze Stitch a quick-and-easy child's cover-up for warm summer days. Serging makes it simple, fun and fast!

By Laura Dollar

Finished size

9–12 months

Materials

- ⅜ yard lightweight woven fabric
  (½ yard for directional prints)
- Threads:
  1 spool rayon
  4 cones serger to match rayon
- Basic sewing supplies and equipment

Cutting

Refer to Cutting Layout.

Note: *Refold fabric so selvages meet in the center.*

Summer Breeze
Cutting Layout

- Cut one front on fold. Mark placement for ties.
- Cut one back on fold. Mark placement for ties.
  Cut slit as indicated on template.

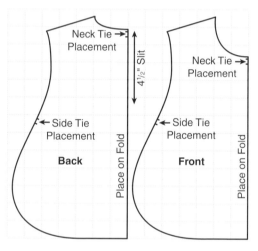

Summer Breeze
Templates
1 square = 1"

Note: *Open fabric to a single layer and cut ties from center.*

- Cut four 1 x 12½-inch bias strips for side ties.
- Cut two 1 x 10½-inch bias strips for neck ties.

Assembly

Use a 4-thread overlock with a wide seam width and medium stitch length for seaming with serger thread in both needles and loopers. Refer to your owner's manual for rolled edge set up. For rolled edge, use rayon thread in the upper looper and matching serger thread in lower looper and needle.

1. Using a 4-thread overlock and right sides together, serge front to back at shoulders. Press seam flat, then toward back.

2. Reset serger for 3-thread rolled edge with rayon thread in upper looper and serger thread in needle and lower looper.

3. Open fabric slit to lay flat in a straight line smoothing excess fabric at the bottom of the slit to the left. Roll the left back neck opening without trimming fabric, turn the corner (refer to page 16) and roll into the slit. As you approach the "V", raise the presser foot as needed to keep the raw edge of the fabric hugging the upper blade. In the "V", with the presser foot in an upright position, refold the fabric to the opposite side so that the fold is behind the presser foot. Roll a few more stitches, and release the fabric. Continue serging in a straight line to the end of the right-hand edge, turn the corner and continue along the neckline without trimming the fabric.

4. To finish the rolled edge seam, stitch over the first several stitches of the rolled edge. Raise the presser foot, and gently pull on the needle thread to loosen the thread on the stitch finger. Slide the fabric and thread off the stitch finger by gently pulling the fabric straight back. Roll another inch of thread. Clip threads.

Apply seam sealant to double stitched rolled edge portion of the edge. Let dry and trim threads.

5. Fold each side tie and neck tie in half lengthwise with wrong sides together. Serge long raw edges together using the same rolled edge and trimming off a scant ⅛ inch of fabric. Apply seam sealant to ends of ties.

6. Fold under a scant ¼ inch on one end of each tie. Position folded ends on wrong sides of front and back as indicated on template. Tack-stitch ends in place by hand or on sewing machine. §

Tips & Techniques

Serge curved edges with a slow, steady speed. Gently turn fabric in front of the presser foot, keeping raw edge of fabric against the upper blade so knife will trim stray threads.

All bias edges are prone to stretching. Take care not to pull fabric while stitching or pressing the long edges of the ties or the curved edges of the top.

Serge Sweet Baby

Yo-yo Baby Quilt

Fast and easy are the buzz words used in creating this delightful baby quilt. Two stitch settings on your serger and precut fabric strips, and you are on your way to quilting.

By Lorine Mason

Finished size
50 x 40 inches

Materials
• 44/45-inch lightweight woven fabric:
      1½ yards print (A)
      1 yard print (B)
      1 yard print (C)
      1½ yards backing
• Quilt batting
• Threads:
      1 cone woolly nylon
      2 or 3 spools serger
• Basic sewing supplies and equipment

Cutting
From print (A) fabric:
• Cut 25 (7 x 7-inch) squares for quilt blocks.
• Cut five 4 x 7-inch rectangles for quilt blocks.
• Cut 16 (4 x 4-inch) circles for yo-yos.

From print (B) fabric:
• Cut one 7 x 45-inch rectangle for top panel.
• Cut three 4 x 45-inch strips for ruffles.
• Cut 16 (4 x 4-inch) circles for yo-yos.

From print (C) fabric:
• Cut 11 (3 x 45-inch) strips for borders.

Note: Backing will be cut after top is pieced.

Assembly
Use a 3- or 4-thread overlock with a ¼-inch-wide seam and medium stitch length, unless otherwise stated. Use polyester or poly/cotton blend thread. Press as you sew. For rolled edge yo-yos, refer to your owner's manual for rolled edge set up. Change the thread to woolly nylon in the upper looper and polyester or poly/cotton blend thread in the needle and lower looper for the rolled edge.

1. Referring to Assembly Diagram, serge quilt blocks and border strips together into rows with a 4-thread overlock. Press and trim border strips even with blocks edges.

2. Serge block rows together using additional border strips. Press and trim even with block edges.

3. Serge another border strip to the top edge of the block unit. Press and trim edges even with block unit.

Serge top panel to top edge of final border strip. Press and trim edges even with quilt.

4. With right sides together, serge ruffle strips together along short edge. Press strips in half lengthwise, wrong sides together. Starting at the right-hand end, mark along the edge of the ruffle using the following measurement sequence: 3 inches, 1½ inches and 1½ inches (Figure 1).

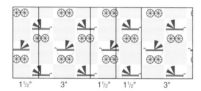

Figure 1

5. Starting once again at the right end of the strip, fold fabric at the first mark to meet the first 1½-inch mark; pin. Fold the second 1½-inch mark back to meet the fold, creating a box pleat; pin. Repeat to the end of the strip. Press (Figure 2).

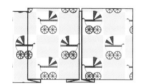

Figure 2

6. Measure 3½ inches down the strip to the center of the first pleat. Undo pleats if necessary to achieve this measurement, trimming away excess fabric. Turn in ½ inch and press well. With right sides together, pin strip to quilt top, starting ½ inch below the top-panel edge. Continue pinning to within ½ inch from the bottom edge of the quilt and trim strip, allowing ½ inch to turn under, similar to the top edge. Repeat along opposite edge of quilt top.

7. Pin quilt backing fabric and quilt batting to the quilt top, right sides together, trimming both layers to fit quilt top. Serge layers together, removing pins as you sew and leaving a 6-inch opening along one side. Turn quilt right side out and press well. Hand-stitch opening closed.

8. Layer two 4-inch circles together, right sides out. Serge layers together using a rolled hem stitch. Using either a sewing machine or hand-stitching, sew a row of gathering stitches ¾ inch from outside edge of circle. Pull gathering thread and wrap around bottom edge of yo-yo.

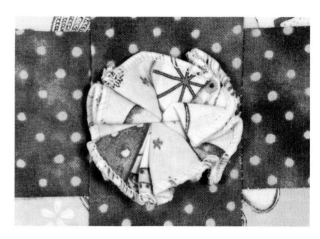

9. Stitching through center back, attach yo-yo to quilt top at intersections of borders, stitching through all layers of the quilt. Sew through quilt multiple times to achieve a secure attachment. **§**

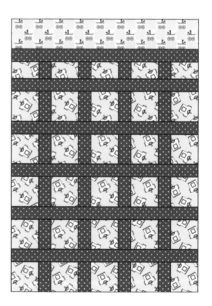

Yo-yo Baby Quilt
Assembly Diagram

Heirloom Baby Bib Use fine cottons and delicate laces to create this beautiful heirloom bib—on your serger!

By Lynn Weglarz

Finished size
Infant

Materials
- ⅜ yard 44/45-inch-wide fine lightweight cotton fabric
- Insertions:
    - ⅜ yard ⅜-inch-wide beading
    - ¾ yard ⅝-inch-wide lace
    - ¾ yard 2-inch-wide embroidered
- 1⅜ yards ¼-inch-wide ribbon
- Optional: water-soluble stabilizer
- Threads:
    - 1 cone woolly nylon to coordinate with fabric
    - 2 cones serger to coordinate with fabric
    - all-purpose to match fabric
- Basic sewing supplies and equipment

Cutting
From lightweight cotton fabric:
- Use template to cut two bibs on fold for lining.
- Cut two 8 x 14-inch rectangles for pintucks.

From lace insertion:
- Cut two 14-inch lengths.

From embroidered insertion:
- Cut two 14-inch lengths.

From ribbon:
- Cut one 14-inch length.
- Cut two 18-inch lengths.

Assembly
Use a 3-thread overlock with a narrow seam width and short stitch length. Use woolly nylon in the upper looper and serger thread in the lower looper and needle. Use a low heat setting when pressing or drying to avoid melting the woolly nylon.

1. With right sides together, serge ⅝-inch-wide lace insertion to each side of beading insertion (Figure 1) with ⅛ to ¼ inch of fabric edge of beading extending beyond the heading of the lace. Press serged seam toward lace.

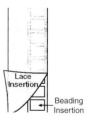

Figure 1

2. Serge 2-inch-wide embroidered insertion to edges of ⅝-inch-wide lace insertion in same manner, allowing needle to catch the heading of the lace. **Note:** *The lace should be just slightly to the right of the needle mark.* Press serged seam toward lace (Figure 2).

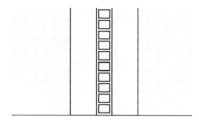

Figure 2

3. To make first pintuck, fold one 8 x 14-inch pintuck piece wrong sides together 1½ to 2 inches from edge of fabric. Butt fabric fold against upper knife, taking care to not cut the fabric. Serge along folded edge. Press seam so woolly nylon shows.

4. Fold fabric again to create a ¾-inch tuck with tuck side of fabric face up and edge of serger foot resting on the pintuck that was just created. Serge close to fold (Figure 3). Press seams so woolly nylon shows. Repeat steps 3 and 4 on both 8 x 14-inch pintuck pieces making a total of 3 pintucks of equal spacing on each piece.

Figure 3

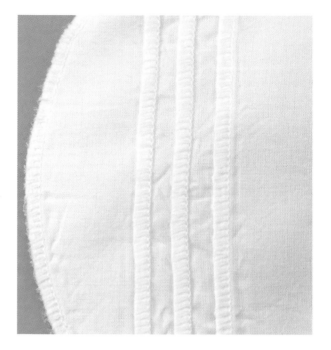

5. With right sides together, serge pintuck piece to each edge of embroidered insertions.

6. Weave the 14-inch length of ribbon through the beading insertion.

7. Use bib lining to cut bib shape from created fabric, centering beading insertion on big lining. With right side facing up, and wrong sides together, baste created-fabric bib to bib linings. Baste ends of 18-inch lengths of ribbon in place as indicated on template.

8. Serge outer edges together, catching ends of ribbon ties in stitching. If needed, apply 1-inch strips of water-soluble stabilizer to support the narrow hem around the curved edges. Remove stabilizer. Press. §

Source: Woolly nylon thread from YLI Corp.

Ribbon Placement

Heirloom Baby Bib
Template
Actual Size

Place on Fold

Quick Cuddly Quilt
Pair up a soft cotton flannel with an even softer minky fabric, then cut simple squares and stitch them together. A serger makes it quick, easy and oh-so cuddly!

By Janis Bullis

Finished size
49 x 67 inches

Materials
- 1½ yards 60-inch-wide heart-embossed minky cuddle fabric
- 4½ yards 45-inch-wide cotton flannel print
- 60 x 80 inches lightweight cotton quilt batting
- Black chenille yarn
- Tapestry needle
- 4 cones serger thread in darkest color of print fabric
- Basic sewing supplies and equipment

Cutting
From minky cuddle fabric:
- Cut six 3-inch strips the width of the fabric for borders.
- Cut 18 (9½ x 9½-inch) squares for quilt blocks.

From flannel fabric:
- Cut two 48-inch panels the width of the fabric for backing.
- Cut 17 (9½ x 9½-inch) squares for quilt blocks.

From chenille yarn:
- Cut 24 (8-inch) lengths.

Assembly
Use a 3- or 4-thread overlock with a ¼-inch wide seam and medium stitch length, trimming very little of fabric. Use polyester or poly/cotton blend thread. Pin and stitch fabrics *wrong* sides together with nap brushed down unless otherwise stated. If desired, seams may be reinforced by adding a straight stitch just outside the overlock.

1. With wrong sides together, serge 14 minky and flannel block units (Figure 1).

Figure 1

2. Serge units together to make seven rows of four blocks each. On four rows, serge a minky block to the right-hand end. On three rows, serge a flannel block to the left-hand end (Figure 2).

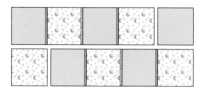

Figure 2

3. Serge the seven completed rows together, alternating blocks (Figure 3) and pushing the minky seam allowance toward the flannel at each intersection.

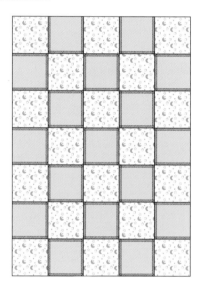

Figure 3

4. Using a tapestry needle, pull each length of chenille yarn through seams at each block intersection and tie in a bow.

5. Serge one long edge of each border.

6. Match the center of one border strip to the center of the short edge of the block unit. Pin and serge border to block unit across edge, pushing minky block seam allowances toward flannel blocks at intersections. Allow ends of border to extend beyond

edges of block unit. Do not trim. Repeat across opposite edge of block unit (Figure 4).

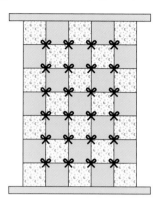

Figure 4

7. Cut one of the remaining border strips in half. With right sides together, join end of one full-length border strip to end of short border strip to create a longer border. Repeat with remaining long and short border strips.

8. Match center of long border strips to center of block unit sides and pin. Serge from edge of block unit to opposite edge, leaving top and bottom borders loose and extending from edges (Figure 5).

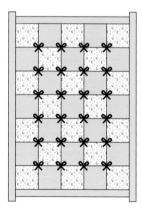

Figure 5

9. At each corner, fold and mark border tails to create a mitered corner (Figure 6). Stitch across mark (Figure 7).

Figure 6

Figure 7

10. With right sides together, serge the selvedge edge of two flannel backing panels together. Layer batting between wrong sides of block unit and backing. Pin flat at each block intersection. Trim batting and backing even with edge of block unit (not border edge).

11. Wrap border to the back side of quilt and pin on right side, catching all layers.

12. Miter-fold corners on back side of quilt and pin. Stitch as before.

13. Use sewing machine to topstitch along serger stitches through all layers on right side of quilt (Figure 8).

Figure 8

14. Hand or machine stitch through all layers at each block intersection. **§**

Source: Minky cuddle fabric from Shannon Fabrics Inc.

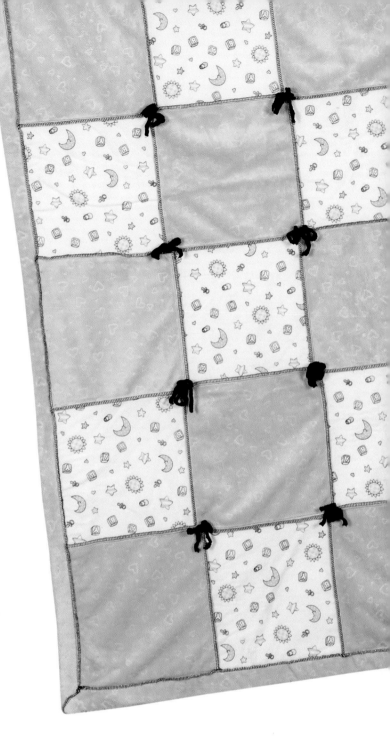

Tips & Techniques

Using safety pins to secure a quilt sandwich (top, batting and back) ensures that pins do not come loose and the quilt sandwich does not shift while completing construction.

Baby Steps Line trendy cotton print with fleece and finish with an overlock stitch to create baby booties as delightful to make as they are to give.

By Pamela Hastings

Finished size

3–6 months

Materials

- ¼ yard cotton print fabric
- ¼ yard lightweight fleece
- 32 inches ⅜-inch-wide grosgrain ribbon
- 3 cones or spools contrasting polyester or poly/cotton blend thread
- Basic sewing supplies and equipment

Cutting

From cotton print:

- Use template (page 40) to cut four bootie fronts, reversing two.
- Cut two 5½ x 4¾-inch rectangles for bootie backs.

From lightweight fleece:

- Use template (page 40) to cut four bootie fronts, reversing two.
- Use template (page 40) to cut two bootie bottoms.
- Cut two 5½ x 4¾-inch rectangles for bootie backs.

From grosgrain ribbon:

- Cut into four 8-inch lengths.

Assembly

Use 3-thread overlock with narrow stitch width and contrasting thread. Use a shorter stitch length for better coverage.

1. For each bootie, place fleece bootie front pieces right sides together and stitch along center front seam using a three-thread overlock stitch. Repeat with cotton print bootie fronts (Figure 1). Press piece open.

Figure 1

2. Place fleece and cotton print bootie fronts wrong sides together, matching raw edges and seam lines. Serge all raw edges. Repeat with bootie back rectangles (Figure 2).

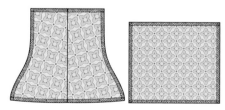

Figure 2

3. Fold top edges of fronts ⅝ inch to inside on fold line. Stitch in place with a straight stitch along overlocked edges.

4. Fold top edges of back 1½ inches to outside. Insert end of ribbon length at each edge. Stitch across edges using a straight stitch along the overlocked edges (Figure 3).

Figure 3

5. With fleece sides together, pin bootie front to bootie bottom matching center seams. Mark center of bootie back on bottom edge. Pin bootie back to

bootie bottom with fleece sides together, matching centers and lapping the front edges of back over sides of bootie front (Figure 4).

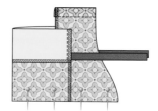

Figure 4

6. Using overlock stitch and a scant ⅛-inch seam allowance, serge front and back to bottom, pushing and guiding with fingers and keeping fabric edges flush.

7. Repeat steps 5 and 6 with second bootie. Tie ribbons in bows on fronts. §

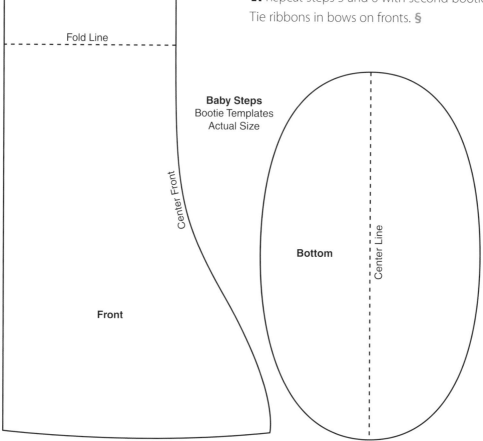

Fold Line

Center Front

Front

Baby Steps
Bootie Templates
Actual Size

Bottom

Center Line

Bow Tie for Baby
Minky fabrics are a great choice for this textured quilt because they are so wonderfully pleasing to touch and simple to serge, making this project a joy to create and a delight to receive!

By Laura Dollar

Finished size
42 x 56 inches

Materials
• 58/60-inch-wide minky dot fabric for blocks and border:
  - ¼ yard pale green
  - ¼ yard light blue
  - ¼ yard soft pink
  - ½ yard white
• 44/45-inch-wide flannel fabric for blocks:
  - 1⅓ yard coordinating print
• Fabric for backing:
  - 1⅝ yards minky dot or flannel
• 3 or 4 cones serger thread
• Basic sewing supplies and equipment

Cutting
From minky dot fabric for blocks and borders:
• Cut 18 (4 x 4-inch) squares each from pale green, light blue and soft pink, for a total 54 blocks.

• Cut two 35½ x 4-inch strips and two 56½ x 4-inch strips from white for borders. ***Note:*** *Cut strips crosswise so nap is smooth crosswise on the strips.*

From flannel fabric for blocks:
• Cut 36 (4 x 4-inch) squares.
• Cut 17 (7½ x 7½-inch) squares.

From fabric for backing:
• Cut one 43 x 56½-inch rectangle. ***Note:*** *If using minky for backing, cut so nap runs lengthwise.*

Block Assembly
Use a 3- or 4-thread overlock with a ¼-inch wide seam and a medium stitch length. Use polyester or poly/cotton blend thread.

Note: *Each block uses three minky squares of the same color and two flannel squares. Make six blocks of each color for a total of 18 bow-tie blocks.*

Before cutting and assembling blocks, see Tips & Techniques on page 47.

1. Place a 4-inch minky block right side up. Fold the next 4-inch minky block in half wrong sides together and position it on top of the first block with the fold lengthwise in the middle of the square and the cut edges aligned on the left (Figure 1).

Figure 1

2. Lay a 4-inch flannel block right side down on top of two minky blocks. Serge across the top edge, catching the top short end of the folded piece in the seam (Figure 2).

Figure 2

3. Place the third minky block right side up on the work surface. Pick up the partially assembled block by the center folded piece, allowing the two sewn blocks to fall away at the seam. Position this folded piece on the third minky block with the cut edges on the left and the lengthwise fold in the center, position as before (Figure 3).

Figure 3

4. Lay another 4-inch flannel block right side down on top of this section and serge across the top as before. The center folded piece will now form the dimensional aspect of the block.

5. Open the center folded piece so the first and second seam meet in the middle and the cut edges are even along the top (Figure 4). Snug the center seams together by having them lay in opposite directions.

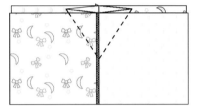

Figure 4

6. Match edges of blocks along this edge on the left and right of the center block. Place pins to secure the positioning. This seam will be stitched straight across. ***Note:*** *It will start out curved while pinned and you will straighten it as you serge.* Open the block and lay it flat to create a 7½-inch 3-dimensional block.

continued on page 47

Cozy Cover Bundle Baby in this attractive and comfortable wrap. Defined legs make transporting in a car seat a snap!

By Dorothy Martin

Finished size

Newborn–6 months

Materials

• 1½ yards 60-inch-wide fleece fabric
• 3 sets No. 10/21mm metal snaps
• 27 inches ⅝-inch-wide grosgrain ribbon
• Threads:
> 2 spools 12-weight multicolored
>   cotton embroidery
> 1 spool coordinating 30-weight multicolored
>   cotton embroidery
> 1 spool of all-purpose to match fleece
• Basic sewing supplies and equipment

Cutting

Enlarge cover template (page 47) as indicated.

From fleece fabric:

• Make sure 60-inch crosswise edge is straight. Fold this crosswise edge over to meet the selvage edge, forming a point at the top (Figure 1). Place template on folded edge with diagonal line on the selvage/cut edge (Figure 2). Cut out cover. Mark darts, fold lines and stitching for legs on wrong side.
• Cut four 2½-inch circles for roses.

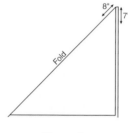

Figure 1   **Figure 2**

Assembly

Use a 3-thread overlock with a medium seam width and stitch length. Use 12-weight variegated thread in the upper and lower loopers and the 30-weight thread in the needle.

1. Stitch darts on sewing machine using straight stitches. Trim ¼ inch from stitching line.

2. Serge perimeter of cover right side up.

3. Fold lower edge to right side on fold line. Straight-stitch on sewing machine to within 1½ inches of fabric edge as indicated on template (Figure 3).

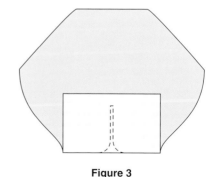

Figure 3

4. Cut legs apart on center line from fold to crotch line. Trim seam to ¼ inch. Clip into curved crotch seam.

5. Turn legs right side out. Use straight stitch on sewing machine to sew side seams and reinforce crotch as indicated on template (Figure 4).

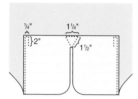

Figure 4

6. Cut six 4½-inch lengths of grosgrain ribbon. Fold in half and join by sewing a zigzag stitch across cut edges to create ribbon tabs. Turn right side out.

7. Referring to Figure 5 for placement, secure ribbon tabs between fleece and snaps. Stitch snaps through all layers.

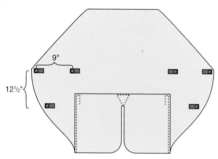

Figure 5

8. Serge perimeter of each rose circle, continuing serge chain at least 36 inches (Figure 6).

Figure 6

9. On sewing machine, baste the serge chain to the circle in a spiral, starting at the edge of the circle and stitching to the center. Stabilize stitching at center (Figure 7).

Figure 7

10. Draw up basting thread from bobbin side to make a free-form rose, drawing the fullness as much as possible to the center of the circle. Manipulate rose with your fingers to get desired look. Tie off.

11. Tack a rose to outside of cover over stitches holding snaps. Tack remaining rose to hood near the neck dart. §

Source: Blendables 12- and 30-weight cotton embroidery thread from Sulky of America.

Tips & Techniques

If desired, replace No. 10/21mm metal snaps with ⅝ x 1-inch rectangles of hook-and-loop tape, or purchased rounds. Omit ribbon tabs.

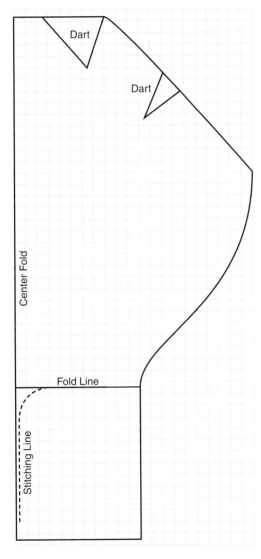

Cozy Cover
Template
1 square = 1"

(labels within template: Dart, Dart, Center Fold, Fold Line, Stitching Line)

Bow Tie for Baby

Continued from page 42

Quilt Assembly

1. Arrange bow-tie and flannel blocks, alternating colors, in seven rows of five blocks each. Serge blocks together in each row, then serge rows together.

2. Serge top and bottom borders, then sides, making sure nap all runs the same direction.

3. Place pieced top and backing right sides together and serge around outer edge, leaving an opening for turning. Turn right side out and slipstitch opening closed. Top-stitch ¼ inch from edge.

4. Stitch around each block by hand or machine to quilt. §

Tips & Techniques

• *When cutting knit fabric like minky, lay the fabric relaxed and flat. Do not pull or stretch the fabric.*

Figure 5

• *If you'd like to have the nap of the finished bow ties in the blocks all going in the same direction when finished, follow the placement guides in Figure 5 as indicated by the arrows.*

Sergeable Wearables

You'll be amazed at how fast you can create custom designed wearables when you use your serger. Try these time-saving designs to make a seasonal wardrobe in days!

Smart Serged Sweatshirt Use your serger to create simple-to-sew sweatshirt remakes. They are fun, fast and so very stylish.

By Lorine Mason

Finished size
Your size

Materials
• Ivory crewneck sweatshirt with inset sleeves
• 44/45-inch lightweight woven fabric:
 ½ yard print (A)
 ½ yard print (B)
 ¼ yard print (C)
 ¼ yard print (D)
• ¼ yard lightweight fusible interfacing
• ½-inch-wide fusible web tape
• 4 buttons
• Decorative belt buckle
• Snap fastener
• 3 or 4 cones matching serger thread
• Painter's tape
• Basic sewing supplies and equipment

Cutting
From print (A) fabric:
• Cut three 4-inch strips the width of the fabric.

From print (B) fabric:
• Cut three 4-inch strips the width of the fabric.

From print (C) fabric:
• Cut two 2-inch strips the width of the fabric.
• Use template (page 52) to cut one collar on fold, adjusting length as needed to fit sweatshirt neckline.

From print (D) fabric:
• Cut two 2-inch strips the width of the fabric.
• Use enlarged template (page 52) to cut one collar on fold, adjusting length as needed to fit sweatshirt neckline, see note on Step 7.

From lightweight fusible interfacing:

• Cut one 2 x 45-inch strip.

• Use enlarged template (page 52) to cut one collar on fold, adjusting length as needed to fit sweatshirt neckline, see note on Step 7.

Assembly

Use a 3- or 4-thread overlock with ¼-inch-wide seam and medium stitch length, unless otherwise stated. Use polyester or poly/cotton blend thread. For a decorative effect, use pearl cotton or baby yarn in upper and lower loopers. Press as you sew.

1. Fold sweatshirt with wrong sides facing, matching shoulder seams at neck intersection. Pin side seams from the bottom rib to the beginning of the armscye (Figure 1). **Note:** *If sweatshirt does not have side seams, continue pinning from the shoulder point to the lower sleeve seam along the armscye.* Lay the sweatshirt flat; lightly pat and smooth sweatshirt toward the center to determine the center front. Mark center front at neck and lower rib edges.

Figure 1

2. Remove pins. Turn sweatshirt to the wrong side, matching side seams. Draw a line to connect markings. Stabilize sweatshirt with painter's tape along center line. Use a long ruler and rotary cutter and mat to open center front. Turn sweatshirt to the right side. (Figure 2). Remove tape.

Figure 2

3. Cut ribbing from neckline, bottom and cuffs, leaving seams attached to sweatshirt. Press ½-inch fusible web tape to the wrong side of sweatshirt along front edges. Turn under ¾ inch along each edge and press.

4. Serge short ends of two 4-inch print (A) strips with right sides together using a diagonal seam. Press seam open. Repeat with 4-inch print (B) strips. Place joined strips with wrong sides together, and serge along bottom edge across the length of the strip.

5. Beginning at the right-hand edge of each strip, measure and mark at 3 inches, 1½ inches and 1½ inches (Figure 3). Repeat the sequence of measurements across the strip. Beginning again at the right-hand end, fold fabric at first mark to meet the first 1½-inch mark; pin. Fold second 1½-inch mark back to meet the first fold, creating a box pleat (Figure 4); pin. Repeat across the strip.

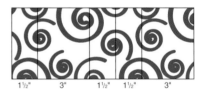

Figure 3

Figure 4

6. Repeat steps 4 and 5 with second set of print (A) and print (B) strips.

7. Cut one pleated strip in half. Cut sweatshirt open at sleeve/side seams, leaving seam allowance attached to sweatshirt (Figure 5 on page 52). Pin the center of one half strip to the right side of sweatshirt at center of sleeve opening edge, matching raw edges. Continue pinning across sleeve opening. Adjust placement of pleats as necessary for a good fit. Serge strip to bottom of sweatshirt sleeve, trimming away

sweatshirt seam allowance (Figure 6). Press seam toward sleeve.

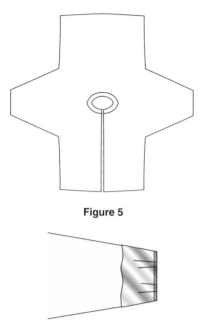

Figure 5

Figure 6

8. With right sides together, serge sweatshirt side/sleeve seams, trimming away sweatshirt seam allowance. Turn sweatshirt to right side and press.

9. Pin center of second pleated strip to right side of sweatshirt at center back along bottom edge, matching raw edges. Continue pinning strip to sweatshirt, being careful not to stretch sweatshirt. Trim ends of strip ½ inch from center front edges

of sweatshirt. Finish short ends of pleated strip with a double ¼-inch hem. **Option:** *Trim ends even with center front of sweatshirt and serge edges to finish.* Serge strip to bottom edge of sweatshirt, trimming off sweatshirt seam allowance. Press seam toward sweatshirt.

10. To create the belt, sew ends of two print (C) 2-inch strips right sides together using a diagonal seam. Repeat with print (D) 2-inch strips. With wrong sides together, serge joined (C) and (D) strips across top and bottom edges. Adjust length of belt, allowing additional length for the belt buckle, and serge ends of belt. Slip end of belt through belt buckle and stitch through all layers to secure.

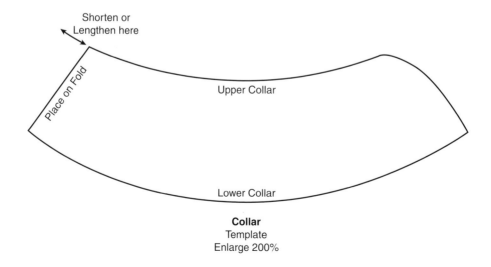

11. Cut remaining length of 2-inch strip in half across the length to make two 1-inch-wide strips. Serge across long raw edges of each 1-inch strip. From these,

Shorten or
Lengthen here

Place on Fold

Upper Collar

Lower Collar

Collar
Template
Enlarge 200%

cut five 1 x 5-inch strips for belt loops. Press under ½ inch at each end of each loop. Position around sweatshirt just above pleated hemline; stitch across top and bottom to secure.

12. Fuse collar interfacing to wrong side of one fabric collar piece. With wrong sides together, serge collar pieces together along upper collar.

13. Pin lower collar to neckline of sweatshirt, gently stretching neckline to fit. Serge collar to sweatshirt, trimming away sweatshirt seam allowance. Press.

14. Mark buttonhole placement. Sew buttonholes on left side. Sew buttons on right side to correspond. Sew a snap fastener at top and bottom of front.

15. Slip belt through belt loops and buckle in front. §

All-Stitched-Up Denim Breathe new life into faded denim by using serger stitches for embellisment.

By Marianne Guy

Finished size

Your size

Materials

- Pattern for straight jacket with front button closure, panel seams, waist seams and full-length sleeves with center and elbow seams*
- 4 pairs misses old jeans
- 2 yards Madras plaid fabric
- 2 (10-yard) spools ⅛-inch-wide satin ribbon to coordinate with Madras plaid
- 2 yards fusible interfacing
- 2 (12-foot) spools ⅜-inch-wide decorative ribbon to coordinate with Madras plaid
- Assorted charms
- Toggle clasps
- Heat-set crystals with applicator wand
- Threads:
    Decorative for embellishing
        (12-weight cotton, rayon, etc.)
    4 cones serger to match decorative threads
- ¼-inch-wide double-sided self-adhesive fusible web tape
- Chenille brush
- Basic sewing supplies and equipment

Model was made using Kwik Sew jacket pattern No. 3129.

Cutting

From denim jeans:

- Follow pattern instructions to cut out jacket pieces Nos. 1, 2, 3, 4, 5, 6, 11, 12, 13 and 14. **Note:** *Make sure to cut a left and right side for each piece and mark backs of pieces with corresponding numbers. Place pattern pieces on top of existing seams, and use garments with different shades of denim for a unique look.*

From Madras plaid fabric:

- Follow pattern instructions to cut out front and back facing pieces No. 9 and No. 10.
- Cut remaining fabric into ¾-inch-wide bias strips the width of the fabric.
- Cut 16 (2½-inch) circles for rosettes.
- Cut 4 (4-inch) squares.

From fusible interfacing:

- Follow pattern instructions to cut out front and back facings pieces No. 9 and No. 10.

Assembly

Use a 3- or 4-thread overlock for stitching and edge finishing inside jacket with polyester or poly/cotton blend thread with a ¼-inch-wide seam and a medium stitch length. Use chain stitch and cover stitch with decorative threads in the loopers for embellishments

and polyester or poly/cotton blend thread in the needle(s). Press as you sew.

1. Sew upper back (pieces No. 5) together on center back seam using sewing machine and ⅝-inch seam allowance. Edge finish and trim seam to ¼ inch.

2. If desired, fuse remnant pieces from jeans, labels, etc., on upper back for embellishment using fusible web tape. On wrong side of upper back, mark where rivets are to avoid stitching over them. With wrong side of upper back fabric up, meander over fabric with chain stitch and/or cover stitch.

3. Cut ten bias strips of plaid the length of the lower back left side (piece No. 6). Layer strips together in pairs evenly spaced across lower back left side and chainstitch down the center of each pair of strips. Use chenille brush to fray edges of strips.

4. On lower back right side (piece No. 6), hold two different colors of ⅛-inch-wide ribbon, crisscrossing them to make a figure 8. Chain-stitch across fabric, catching ribbon at each crossing to hold in place. Add bias strips at corners; brush edges to fray.

5. Sew upper front left side pieces together (pieces No. 1 and No. 2) on sewing machine using a ⅝-inch seam allowance. Edge finish and trim seam to ¼ inch. With wrong side of fabric up, meander over fabric using a chain stitch and/or cover stitch. Layer four rosette circles together and position on fabric; stitch in center using sewing machine. Brush to fray edges.

6. Sew upper front right side (pieces No. 1 and No. 2) in same manner as left. Using a cover stitch and chain stitch, meander over fabric wrong side up. For additional decorative effect, insert a ⅛-inch-wide ribbon through the coverstitch.

7. Embellish lower left front side (piece No. 3) by fusing on a jeans back pocket and topstitching using sewing machine. Tack a piece of plaid inside.

8. Embellish lower front right side (piece No. 4) by fusing four rows of decorative ribbon on a slant. Meander over fabric, wrong side up, using the chain stitch.

9. Chain-stitch over lower front left side (piece No. 3) right side up. Place the four 4-inch squares vertically across piece, overlapping corners, and chain-stitch down the center, with right side of fabric up. Brush edges of squares to fray.

10. Fuse decorative ribbon diagonally and vertically on lower front right side (piece No. 4). Chain-stitch over fabric, wrong side up.

11. Sew sleeves together (pieces No. 11, No. 12, No. 13 and No. 14) using sewing machine and ⅝-inch seam allowance. Edge finish and trim seam to ¼-inch. Meander over each sleeve using cover stitch, with fabric wrong side up. Crisscross layers of plaid bias strips over each sleeve and sew down the center of each; brush edges to fray.

12. Add additional embellishments such as labels, tags, pockets, crystals, etc., as desired and available.

13. Fuse interfacing to plaid facings. Serge outer edges to finish.

14. Assemble jacket following pattern instructions. ***Option:*** *Cut off 1-inch hem allowance and sew on jeans waistband. Reattach belt loops.*

15. Sew on toggle clasps for buttons. §

Sources: Jacket pattern No. 3129 from Kwik Sew Pattern Co. Inc.; Steam-A-Seam 2 double-stick fusible web tape from The Warm Company.

Rolled Around Tee Add rolled edge tabs around your neckline to hold your scarf in place. Slide the scarf slide through the tabs, hang loose in front, tie at the side or trail down your back, Isadora Duncan style.

By Lynn Weglarz

Finished size
Your size

Materials
- Basic T-shirt pattern*
- Stretch-knit fabric as indicated on pattern
- 44/45-inch-wide fabric:
    ⅛-yard lightweight woven for tabs
    ½ yard sheer for scarf
- Threads:
    1 cone woolly nylon to coordinate with scarf and tabs
    2 cones 100 percent polyester to coordinate with scarf and tabs
    All-purpose to match T-shirt
- Water-soluble stabilizer
- Optional: ½-inch-wide paper-backed fusible tape
- Basic sewing supplies and equipment

Kwik Sew pattern No. 2619 was used for model project.

Cutting
From stretch-knit fabric:
- Cut T-shirt front, back, neckband and sleeves following pattern instructions.

From lightweight woven fabric:
- Cut five 1¼ x 6-inch pieces for tabs.

From sheer fabric:
- Cut two pieces each 8 inches by the width of the fabric for scarf.

From water-soluble stabilizer:
- Cut enough 1-inch-wide strips to go around raw edges of scarf.

Assembly
Use a 4-thread overlock with polyester thread to assemble T-shirt. Adjust the 4-thread overlock to a ¼-inch wide seam and a medium stitch length. Use 3-thread narrow hem with woolly nylon in upper looper and cone thread in lower looper and needle for decorative serging over the elastic. Adjust the 3-thread overlock to a narrow seam width and short stitch length.

1. Refer to pattern instructions to assemble T-shirt up to neckband attachment.

2. Using a 3-thread narrow hem on serger with wooly nylon in the upper looper and cone thread in the

lower looper and needle, serge around edges of each tab, trimming tab width slightly to measure 1 inch.

3. With right sides together, evenly space tabs at the neckline: one at center back, two at shoulder seams and two in front (Figure 1).

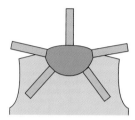

Figure 1

4. Following pattern directions, quarter-mark neckband and neckline with pins. Matching pins, serge neckband to T-shirt, catching ends of tabs in stitching. Press neckline seam to body of shirt and press tabs toward neckband. Topstitch seam.

5. Bring loose ends of tabs to inside of shirt, placing serged ends of tabs slightly over serged edge of neckband (Figure 2). Pin. Topstitch a second row of stitching, catching ends of tabs in stitching.

Figure 2

6. Finish T-shirt as directed in pattern. ***Optional:*** *At sleeve hems and bottom hem, fuse lightweight paper-backed fusible web in hem area. Stitch hems in place.*

7. Adjust the serger for a narrow 3-thread overlock. With right sides together, serge short edges of scarf pieces together. Press. Adjust serger to rolled edge. Place strips of stabilizer under raw edges of scarf and serge edges. Remove excess stabilizer. §

Sources: T-shirt pattern No. 2619 from Kwik Sew Pattern Co. Inc.; woolly nylon and polyester thread from YLI Corp.; Sulky Solvy water-soluble stabilizer from Sulky of America; Lite Steam-A-Seam 2 from The Warm Company.

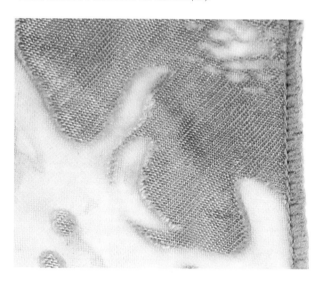

Tips & Techniques

For tucked in shirt, hem bottom edge with a 4-thread serge to eliminate bulk and seam show-through. For sleeves and outside worn hems, fold fabric as needed for a blind hem, and serge into place.

Trim a Tee Cover lengths of narrow elastic with different-color overlock stitches, and then braid together to create a decorative stretch trim!

By Janis Bullis

Finished size
Your size

Materials
- Purchased T-shirt with V-neck
- 6–9 yards ⅛-inch-wide flat braided elastic
- 3 (⅜-inch) shank buttons
- 3 cones each 3 different colors serger thread
- Basic sewing supplies and equipment

Cutting
From elastic:
- Measure the neckline and each sleeve hem. Add 9 inches to each measurement. Cut three lengths of elastic for each.

Assembly
Use a 3-thread overlock with a seam set wide enough to cover the elastic trim. Sample garment uses a medium length, but adjust the length to your preference. A shorter stitch length will provide more coverage of the elastic. Use three spools of polyester or poly/cotton blend thread of the same color.

1. Raise the presser foot. Slide the strip of elastic next to the upper blade. Lower the presser foot and start to serge, being careful not to trim the elastic. Continue serging until the elastic is encased in thread. Sew off the elastic strip. Clip thread. Change thread color, and repeat for each remaining strip of elastic to create three elastic/thread strips for each section of shirt to be trimmed.

2. Pin tail ends of three different colors together and stitch to secure. Braid lengths together and stitch opposite end to secure. Repeat for each section.

3. Fold trim in half. Beginning at center of V-neck, pin the center of the trim into a small loop without twisting braid. Continue pinning braid to center back of neckline along seam. Leave tail ends unpinned (Figure 1).

Figure 1

4. Set sewing machine for bar-tack stitch or medium-width, short-length zigzag stitch. Tack braid to shirt approximately every inch, lifting the presser foot and jumping to the next location each time. Trim jump threads on right and wrong sides of shirt.

5. Mark braid tails at joining and stitch a seam in the braid (Figure 2). Trim tail ends and stitch braid to shirt. Stitch button to shirt in center of loop.

Figure 2

6. Beginning at center of a sleeve hem, create a loop in the braid. Pin and tack braid to sleeve at hemline (Figure 3).

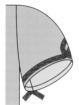

Figure 3

7. Seam tail ends and complete tacking. Stitch button to shirt at loop as before. §

Pintuck Shirt Set your serger for a 3-thread overlock with matching or contrasting thread to create simple-to-serge pintucks.

By Nancy Estep

Finished size

Your size

Materials

• Purchased shirt pattern with front and back yokes
• Fabric as indicated on pattern, less ⅜ yard
• Additional ½ yard of same fabric for pintucking
• Notions as indicated on pattern
• 3–4 cones serger thread to match fabric
• Basic sewing supplies and equipment

Pintucking

1. Prewash and press ½ yard fabric for pintucking. Using water-soluble pen, mark straight lines parallel to the selvage (on grain) ¾ inch apart (Figure 1).

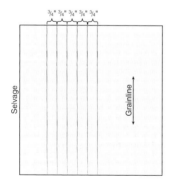

Figure 1

2. Set serger for 3- or 4-thread overlock with a narrow seam width and medium stitch length. Fold and press fabric on marked line and place fold under the foot.

Butt fold against upper blade, and serge without cutting fabric. Continue across fabric. Serge off end of fabric, clip tails and repeat until block of fabric is serged.

3. Mark tucked fabric again, drawing straight lines perpendicular to tucks 1½ inches apart (Figure 2).

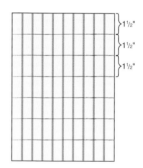

Figure 2   **Figure 3**

4. Set sewing machine for a bar tack. Working left to right, fold the first row of tucks into each other and stitch at each line. When completed, fold next row of tucks in opposite direction and bar tack across (Figure 3). Work across all rows in this manner.

Cutting & Assembly

1. Cut yoke fronts and back from pintucked fabric. Cut remaining shirt pieces from remaining fabric.

2. Assemble shirt following pattern instructions. §

Rectangle to Jacket
Simple shapes are great for serging one-of-a-kind creations. This jackets serges rectangles together to create a sensational low-sew jacket.

By Suzy Seed

Finished size
Your size

Materials
• 56-inch lightweight woven fabric with a soft drape:
- 1½–2 yards print
- ⅜ yard coordinating solid
• 4 or 5 cones serger thread
• Basic sewing supplies and equipment

Preparation
Record measurements as follows:

Back width: Measure upper back across shoulders for back width; add 12 inches (example: 16 + 12 = 28 inches).

Front width: For front measurement, divide the back measurement in half and subtract 2½ inches, rounding down to the nearest whole number (example: 28 ÷ 2 = 14 - 2½ = 11½, rounded down = 11 inches).

Back length: Determine desired back length from shoulders; subtract 2 inches (example: 30 - 2 inches = 28 inches).

Sleeve length: Allow 10–14½ inches for sleeve length, depending on size; subtract 2 inches (example 14½ - 2 = 12½ inches).

Cutting
***Note:** Tearing is recommended.*

From print fabric:
• Tearing *across the width* of the fabric, tear three 4½-inch strips the width of the fabric for sleeve bands and bottom band (Figure 1).
• Tearing *across the width* of the fabric, tear one piece the sleeve length measurement (Figure 1). ***Note:** This will make both sleeves.*
• Tearing *across the width* of the fabric, tear one piece the back length measurement (example: 28 inches) for back and fronts (Figure 1). Open fabric piece for back and fronts. Measure from one selvage edge and tear *across the length* of the fabric as follows:

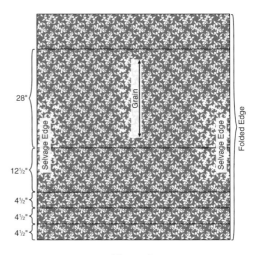

Figure 1

• Tear two pieces the front width for fronts (Figure 2).

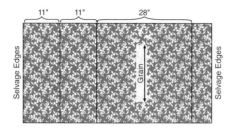

Figure 2

• Tear one piece the back width for back (Figure 2). Fold back in half along lengthwise grain, wrong sides together. Measure 1–1¼ inches from top raw edge at center fold. Beginning at center-fold mark, cut across top raw edge, tapering to nothing at outer edges (Figure 3).

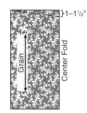

Figure 3

From solid fabric:
• Tear two 4½-inch strips across the width of the solid fabric for front band.

Tips & Techniques

For loosely woven fabric, serge over a piece of twill tape or ribbon for added strength. The twill stabilizes the seam keeping it form stretching as the garment is worn.

Assembly

Use a 4- or 5-thread overlock with ¼-inch wide seam and medium stitch length, unless otherwise stated. Use polyester or poly/cotton blend thread. Press as you sew.

1. With right sides together, serge fronts to back at shoulders, beginning at outer selvage edges and stitching toward neck opening. Press seams toward back.

2. Mark center of each sleeve. With right sides together, pin each sleeve center at shoulder seam. Serge each sleeve to front/back armsyce. Press seam toward sleeve. With right sides together and edges even, serge underarm/side seams. Press.

3. Cut sleeve bands to fit lower edges of sleeves, plus ½-inch seam allowance. Serge short edges of each band together; press in half lengthwise with wrong sides together. With right sides together, serge raw edges to bottoms of sleeves.

4. Cut bottom band to fit bottom of jacket. Press in half lengthwise with wrong sides together. With right sides together, serge raw edges to bottom edge of jacket.

5. With right sides together, serge short edges of front band strips together. Press in half lengthwise with wrong sides together. Press under ¼ inch on one long edge.

6. Open band. Position seam at center back of jacket, right sides together and raw edges even. Serge unpressed edge of band to fronts and neckline. Press seam toward band.

7. Fold short ends of band, right sides together, and serge across bottom ends, even with bottom edge of bottom band. Turn band to right side. Fold pressed edge of band to cover serging, fuse or hand-stitch folded edge in place over serged seam. §

Puzzle Blouse

Make this simple-to-serge puzzle blouse in about twenty minutes, after you make your first one. You'll love this pattern once you figure out the puzzle.

By Suzy Seed

Finished size

Your size

Materials

• 1–1½ yards 44/45-inch lightweight woven fabric
• 3 or 4 cones of serger thread
• Basic sewing supplies and equipment

Cutting & Assembly

Use a 3- or 4-thread overlock with ¼-inch wide seam

Tips & Techniques

• *Model project is about as long as it is wide. If you wish to make a longer top, start with a longer piece of fabric.*

• *Folding fabric with wrong sides together will have stitches on right side of finished top. Fold fabric with right sides together if you prefer stitches not to show.*

and medium stitch length, unless otherwise stated. Use polyester or poly/cotton blend thread. Press as you sew.

1. Take your high bust and hip measurements (Figure 1). **Notes:** *If measurement (example: 33½) is between bust sizes (example: 32–34), use smaller bust size, 32, as measurement, due to the stretch of the bias fabric. If wider at hips, use hip measurement.* Straighten one raw edge of fabric yardage. Measure from selvage edge along the straightened raw edge, to desired width measurement. Tear the fabric this width. To determine the length of the fabric, use the width measurement from above and measure along the selvage. Tear from selvage edge to torn edge to create a fabric square.

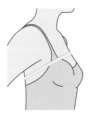

Figure 1

2. Holding fabric with selvages on each end and wrong sides together, fold in half, matching raw edges (Figure 2). Trim selvage from fabric.

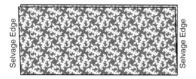

Figure 2

3. Serge across each end (Figure 3).

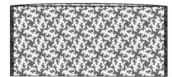

Figure 3

4. Lay stitched piece flat on work surface with folded edge closest to you. Lift folded edge at the corner and fold up to raw edges, forming a bias fold (Figure 4). At raw edges, pin through one layer of fabric only to mark end of stitched edge.

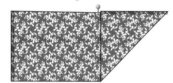

Figure 4

5. At raw edges, lift top layer of fabric at pin and pull raw edges together to form one long seam. Serge across this edge. ***Note:*** *This will create a double-layered square/rectangle with no openings.*

6. Shake out stitched piece with serging on the front to find the grain. Slit open bottom edge with scissors, taking care not to cut through previous stitching (Figure 5). Reshake and lay flat.

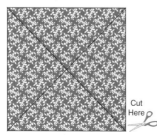

Figure 5

7. Measure 8 or 9 inches from top folded edge on each side for armholes (Figure 6). User scissors to slit open armholes.

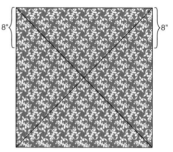

Figure 6

8. Fold blouse in half, matching armholes and aligning folds at sides with seams (front of blouse) inside. Measure and mark blouse back across folded edge 3 to 4 inches from center fold, then 1½ inches from top on center fold for back neckline (Figure 7a). Cut curved opening on back of blouse for back neckline. Refold blouse in half, matching armholes and aligning folds at sides with seams inside. Cut front neckline 2 to 3 inches deeper at center front (Figure 7b). Try on blouse and enlarge neck opening if needed.

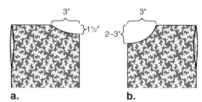

Figure 7

9. Serge around armholes, bottom edge and neckline to finish. §

Tailored for Me Oxford

Customize a man's well-preserved Oxford shirt to your tastes by cutting and adding feminine elements such as lace trim, decorative buttons and flirty fabric!

By Zoe Graul

Finished size
Your size

Materials
- Man's Oxford shirt
- ½ yard 44/45-inch-wide crinkle-type fabric*
- 2 yards 1½-inch-wide lace
- 2 yards ⅜-inch-wide flat trim
- 3 or 4 cones of matching serger thread
- Covered-button forms to fit shirt buttonholes
- Optional: snap or hook-and-loop fastener
- Basic sewing supplies and equipment

Model project used a size large shirt. Amount of fabric will vary depending on size of shirt used.

Instructions
Use a 3- or 4-thread overlock with ¼-inch-wide seam and a medium stitch length. Use polyester or poly/cotton thread. Refer to your owner's manual for rolled edge set up. For a decorative effect, try using a variegated thread in lower looper when rolling.

1. Remove shirt pocket, collar buttons and top button on collar stand. Wash and dry shirt. Try on shirt. With pins, mark bustline and desired finished length of shirt.

2. Divide the distance between the pins approximately in half to determine where the fabric ruffle will start (Figure 1). Add ½ inch for seam allowances and mark with a pin. This is where the shirt bottom will be cut off (6 inches on model project).

Figure 1

3. Measure from the middle pin to the bottom pin. Add ¾ inch. Record for ruffle length.

4. Place shirt flat on tabletop and fold shirt at middle pin (Figure 2), making sure fold is even. Cut along fold. Measure the cut edge, including the placket, and record for ruffle width.

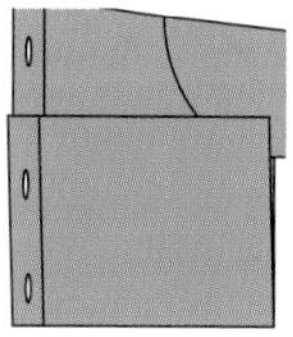

Figure 2

5. Cut the collar from the collar stand, cutting as close to the collar stand as possible. Measure the placket front from the collar stand to cut edge. Cut two lengths of lace this length plus 2 inches. Pin one piece of lace just to the left of the buttons, starting

high enough so the top of the lace is above the bottom stitching on the collar stand. The inside edge of the lace should just cover the original stitching line. Straight stitch close to inside edge of lace. Trim lace to just above the bottom stitching on the collar stand.

6. Repeat on the placket side, but place the inside edge of lace under the placket (Figure 3). ***Note:*** *A zipper foot will make stitching easier.*

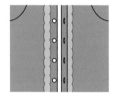

Figure 3

7. Cut a piece of lace the length of the collar stand plus 6 inches. Place over the collar stand. At one end, fold lace back 2 inches (Figure 4). Pin bottom edge of lace over the bottom stitching line of the color stand. Repeat at opposite end of collar stand. Stitch along bottom edge of lace, catching folded-back lace at ends. Hand-tack ends of lace at top of collar stand to hold in place.

Figure 4

8. Referring to steps 3 and 4 for ruffle length and width measurements, add 3–6 inches to the width measurement for front edge hems and ease. Make a gathering stitch ½ inch from top edge of ruffle. Refer to owner's manual for rolled-edge set up and hem front edges and bottom edges with a rolled edge.

9. Pin ruffle to bottom of shirt, right sides together and raw edges even, easing in gathers. Set serger for a 3- or 4-thread overlock, sew raw edges together; remove gathering stitches and press seam allowance up. Beginning on button side of placket, at inside of lace, pin and sew flat trim just above seam line, folding ends under ½ inch. Tack ruffle seam allowance in place as needed.

10. Pin tucks closed above the cuffs on the sleeves. Cut cuffs from sleeves. Try on shirt and measure desired length of sleeves. Add ¾ inch to difference

Tips & Techniques

• *To get the width of lace needed, you can cut a piece of lace in half following the design line (Figure 5).*

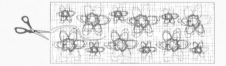

Figure 5

• *If a closer color match is desired, cotton lace can be dyed. Fabric dye, tea or coffee can be used.*

• *If the shirt is a bit too large, take a couple of tucks where darts are usually placed and at the back. Topstitch the tucks for about 1 inch to stay with the Oxford look.*

• *If a shorter sleeve length is desired, create a couple topstitched horizontal pleats starting above the sleeve placket.*

between desired sleeve length and length to edge of cut sleeve. Record for length of sleeve ruffle. Measure around raw edge of sleeve from one placket edge to the other, adding 2 inches for ease and hems. Record. Cut two sleeve ruffles using these measurements. Hem, gather and serge ruffles to bottoms of sleeves in same manner as for shirt ruffle. Press seam allowance up. Topstitch close to ruffle edge.

11. Remove buttons from shirt placket and sleeves. Cover button forms with fabric following manufacturer's instructions. Sew covered buttons to front placket and sleeves. Add a snap or hook-and-loop fastener at bottom and top of front placket and sleeve edge if needed. **§**

Serge Simple Shirt
Basic lines, optional darts for waist shaping and long sleeves make this a fundamental pattern to suit your wardrobe for years.

By Brenda Bornyasz for Brensan Studios

Finished size
Your size

Materials
• Purchased shirt pattern with front and back darts, collar, back yoke, straight sleeves and shallow sleeve cap*
• Lightweight woven fabric as indicated on pattern
• Lightweight woven interfacing as indicated in pattern
• 5 (⅝-inch) buttons
• 4 cones of serger thread
• Basic sewing supplies and equipment

Model project was made using Brensan Studios Sew Simple Shirt No. BSS113.

Cutting

From lightweight woven fabric:
• Cut fronts, back, sleeves, collar, collar facing, front facings, back yoke facing and back yoke as indicated in pattern. Transfer all markings to wrong sides of fronts and back.

From interfacing:
• Cut front facings and collar as indicated in pattern.

Assembly
Use a 4-thread overlock with a ¼-wide seam and medium length, trimming ¼ inch. Use polyester or poly/cotton blend thread. Press as you sew.

1. Serge darts in shirt fronts and back by folding along the center of the dart with right sides together from point to point. Trim as necessary. Use a bodkin to weave thread tail into dart at point.

2. Place interfacing on front facing with wrong sides together. Serge long curved edges together. Turn wrong sides together and press. Trim remaining raw edge of interfacing by ½-inch so it will not be caught in stitching. With right sides together, place front interfacing against front. Serge straight edge, turn facing to inside and press (Figure 1).

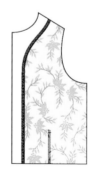 

Figure 1   Figure 2

3. Place right sides of yoke and back together (Figure 2). Place yoke facing with right side against wrong side of back. Serge through all three layers.

4. Pin or baste front to back yoke at shoulder seams, right sides together. Roll up shirt back and fronts. Pull yoke and yoke facing pieces forward so shoulder seams meet right sides together (Figure 3). Pin or baste and serge shoulder seam through all layers: yokes, turning yoke. Press seams flat.

Figure 3

5. Place collar interfacing on wrong side of one collar piece. Place fabric collars right sides together and serge long edge (Figure 4). Turn serged seam onto fabric at collar point and serge from corner point to neck point on both short ends. Turn collar right side out and press. Use a point-turner as needed to shape collar points.

Figure 4

6. Pin collar to back, matching centers (Figure 5a). Turn front facing back at seam, covering collar. Turn facing back ¼ inch to meet shoulder seam on both sides (Figure 5b). Serge collar and facings to shirt. Turn facing and press. Hand-tack facing to shoulder seam.

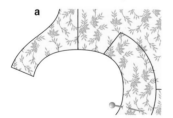

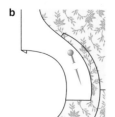

Figure 5

7. With right sides together, matching notches and shoulder seam, serge sleeve to shirt body. Press seam toward body of shirt. Topstitch into place (Figure 6).

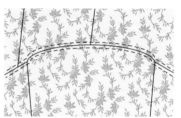

Figure 6

8. Matching notches and sleeve seam right sides together with raw edges even, serge side and underarm seam together.

9. To hem shirt body, fold front facing back, right sides together with front at shirt bottom; pin. Turn serged seam from front facing and front forward. Pin, and repeat for opposite side. Serge bottom of shirt body, removing pins before serging. Turn facing and shirt with wrong sides together; mark and pin hem depth as desired. Topstitch into place.

10. To hem sleeve edge, fold hem as for a blind hem (Figure 7), and serge through all three layers.

Figure 7

11. Follow pattern instructions for stitching buttonholes on right shirt front. Sew buttons on left shirt front. §

Source: Sew Simple Shirt pattern No. BSS113 from Brensan Studios.

Princess P.J.s
Serged-to-perfection perky pink pajamas in a poodle print will make any princess pleased as punch—as long as there are no peas under the mattress.

By Barbara Rezac

Finished size
Your size

Materials
- Purchased pajama pattern with short sleeves, back yoke, capri-length pants and front pocket*
- Fabric sufficient for pieces as indicated in cutting instructions below:
    - bright mottled (A)
    - coordinating print (B)
    - contrasting mottled (C)
- Fusible interfacing as indicated in pattern
- Notions as indicated in pattern
- 4 or 5 cones of serger thread
- Basic sewing supplies and equipment

Kwik Sew pattern No. 3553 was used for model project.

Pattern Preparation
- Cut 2½ inches from bottom edge of sleeve pattern.
- Cut 3¼ inches from bottom edge of capri-length pant leg.

- For elastic casing, check position of fold on pattern. Be sure there is the width of the elastic plus 1 inch beyond the fold.

Cutting

From (A) fabric:
- Use pattern pieces to cut shirt front, shirt back, sleeves and one pocket.
- Cut one 6½-inch strip the width of the fabric for pants cuffs.
- Cut one 1½ x 5-inch piece for flat trim on shirt pocket.

From (B) fabric:
- Use pattern pieces to cut pants, one pocket, shirt yoke, collar and front facings.
- Cut one 5-inch strip the width of the fabric for sleeve cuffs.
- Cut one 1½ x 5-inch piece for flat trim on pants pocket.

From (C) fabric:
- Use pattern piece to cut one yoke lining.
- Cut two 1½-inch strips the width of the fabric for flat trim on sleeves and pant legs.
- Cut two 2 x 5-inch strips for pocket cuffs.

From fusible interfacing:
- Use pattern pieces to cut front facing.
- Use pattern piece to cut one collar.

Assembly

Use 4- or 5-thread overlock with ¼-inch wide seam and medium stitch length, unless otherwise stated. Use polyester or poly/cotton blend thread. Press as you sew.

Pockets

1. Press flat trim for shirt pocket in half lengthwise, wrong sides together. Place across top edge of shirt pocket with top raw edges even (Figure 1).

Figure 1

2. Press pocket cuff in half lengthwise, wrong sides together. Open fold. With right side of fabric toward flat trim, place a single layer of shirt-pocket cuff on top of pocket. Serge seam (Figure 2). Serge opposite edge of cuff to finish edge.

Figure 2

3. Fold cuff right sides together so serging on free edge of cuff is just below seam joining cuff and flat trim. Serge across ends of cuff and perimeter of pocket (Figure 3). Turn cuff right side out. Using serger stitching as a guide, fold under seam allowance on edges of pocket (Figure 4). Stitch in the ditch at bottom of cuff.

Figure 3

Figure 4

4. Repeat steps 1–3 for pants pocket.

Pants

1. With right sides together, serge front and back pants leg down outer leg seam. Repeat with remaining pants leg.

2. Position pants pocket centered over side seam on right pants leg at approximate knee level. Topstitch in place.

3. With right sides together, match right front pants leg to left front pants leg. Serge front rise approximately 6 inches from waist to inner leg seam.

4. Press top (waist) edge under the width of the elastic plus ⅜ inch. Turn folded edge the same width

Tips & Techniques

It's easy to turn a sewing pattern into a serger pattern by following these simple tricks.

• Trim the pattern's seam allowances from ⅝ inch to ¼ inch as you cut the pattern from the fabric yardage.

• Plan the sewing order of the pattern so that you serge long continuous seams (legs, arms and body) first, then serge hems and waistbands.

• When serging a waist band, be sure to leave an opening for elastic (just like when sewing on your conventional machine).

• When serging collar pieces together, serge the long seam first with right sides together. Fold the serged edge to the underside of the collar, and serge each short seam from the long stitched seam to the opposite open edges. Use the same method to serge cuff pieces together. This will give the collar or cuff a perfect corner every time and eliminate the need to trim the seams prior to turning.

back to right side. Serge across, catching raw edge of fabric and fold to form casing (Figure 5). **Note:** *It is okay to trim off the fold.* Insert elastic into casing and adjust to size. Baste ends to secure.

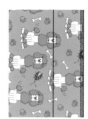

Figure 5

5. Press (C) fabric flat trim in half lengthwise with wrong sides together. Measure width of pant legs at bottom edge. Cut two lengths of flat trim this length. Place on bottoms of pants legs, right sides together and raw edges even.

6. Using same measurement, cut two lengths of (A) fabric strips for pants cuffs. Press in half lengthwise with wrong sides together and place over flat trim on each leg, right sides together and raw edges even (Figure 6). Serge seams.

Figure 6

7. With right sides together, serge inner leg seam on each pants leg, matching ends of cuff and trim. Stitch a bar tack at leg bottom to hold seam to one side.

8. Place one leg inside the other, right sides together. Complete serging the rise, from front waist to back waist catching elastic to secure ends at center back waist. Stitch a bar tack at waist to hold seam to one side.

Pajama Shirt

1. Fuse interfacing to front facings and collar as instructed in pattern. Serge-finish outer edges of front facings.

2. Topstitch shirt pocket to left front as indicated in pattern.

3. Place right side of yoke lining to wrong side of shirt back. Place right side of yoke to right side of shirt back (Figure 7). Serge layers together.

Figure 7

4. With right sides together, pin shirt fronts to yoke at shoulders (Figure 8a). Roll up shirt front and yoke (Figure 8b), then pin right side of yoke lining to wrong side of shirt front at shoulders, matching raw edges (Figure 8c). Serge shoulder seams (Figure 8d). Pull shirt right side out through one armhole.

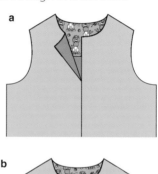
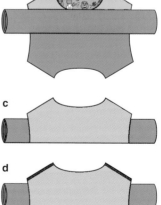

Figure 8

5. With right sides together, pin front facings to shirt front, matching center front raw edges. Serge seams. Turn facings to inside and press. Understitch facing on facing side below roll line of lapel, and on shirt side in lapel area. **Note:** *To understitch, open seam flat. Straight stitch close to seam, catching serged seam allowance underneath.*

6. Fold interfaced collar right sides together and serge short ends. Turn right side out. Press. Roll collar to one side (Figure 9). Baste raw neckline edges together (Figure 10). **Note:** *Raw edges will no longer be even.*

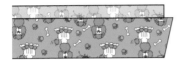

Figure 9

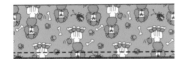

Figure 10

7. Turn front facing over shirt front, right sides together. At top edge of center front seam, fold seam allowance over directly on the needle stitching line (Figure 11). Keep center front seam folded as you serge neckline seam.

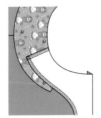

Figure 11

8. Cut and serge sleeve flat trim and sleeve cuffs to bottoms of sleeves, referring to steps 5 and 6 for pants.

9. Pin or baste sleeves to shirt as instructed in pattern. Serge by placing sleeve down on feed teeth and using differential feed to ease in sleeve fullness as needed.

10. With right sides together, match raw edges of shirt body, underarm seams, and raw edges of sleeves, piping and cuffs. Serge. Stitch a bar tack at bottom of sleeve cuff to hold seam to one side.

11. Serge bottom raw edge of shirt. Press hem up to crease (Figure 12a). Turn front facings back with right side of facings to right side of shirt fronts (Figure 12b). Straight-stitch hems across facings (Figure 12c). Trim out bulk. Turn facings to inside. Coverstitch hem in place, or straight stitch on sewing machine.

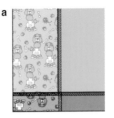

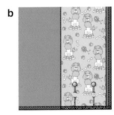

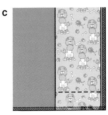

Figure 12

12. Mark and stitch buttonholes as indicated in pattern. Sew on buttons to correspond. §

Source: Pattern No. 3553 from Kwik Sew Pattern Co. Inc.

Fast & Breezy Skirt Use various serger stitches to stitch a simple skirt from top to bottom!

By Lynn Weglarz

Finished size
Your size

Materials
• Purchased pattern for 8-panel elastic-waist skirt*
• Fabric and notions as indicated on pattern
• Threads:

    1 cone woolly nylon to coordinate with fabric

    2 cones 100 percent polyester to coordinate with fabric

    Spool all-purpose to match fabric

• Basic sewing supplies and equipment

Model project was made using Kwik Sew pattern No. 3231.

Cutting & Assembly
Use a 3-thread overlock with a narrow seam width and medium stitch length, unless otherwise stated. *Sew wrong sides together.* Use woolly nylon in upper looper and polyester thread in lower looper and needle. Use a cool iron to avoid melting the woolly nylon thread.

1. Cut out skirt panels following pattern instructions.

2. Straight-stitch skirt panels together on sewing machine. **Note:** *Seams will be on the outside of the skirt.*

3. Serge all seams to ¼ inch and press to one side so wooly nylon stitching shows.

4. Following pattern instructions, overlap ends of elastic ⅜ inch and stitch together. Quarter-mark elastic circle and waistline edge. Matching quarter marks, with elastic on top of the right side of the waistline edge, serge elastic in place (Figure 1).

Figure 1

5. Turn elastic to wrong side of skirt. Match quarter marks, and stretching elastic to fit waistline edge, topstitch elastic in place along bottom edge of elastic (Figure 2).

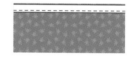

Figure 2

6. Even out hem edge if necessary. Serge hem edge to finish. Press. §

Sources: Skirt pattern 3231 from Kwik Sew Pattern Co. Inc.; Wooly nylon thread from YLI Corp.

Tips & Techniques

Position elastic on top of fabric and butt both layers against the upper knife to prevent cutting the elastic. Take a couple of stitches into elastic before stretching it, and hold all layers behind the foot as you serge.

Flatlock Fleece
Easy modifications to a purchased pattern and the simplicity of flatlock stitches make designing a one–of–a–kind vest a fleece of cake!

By Barbara Rezac

Finished size
Your size

Materials
• Purchased vest pattern with front yoke, forward side seams with cut-on pockets, stand-up collar and contrasting binding*
• Polar fleece fabric:
> print (see cutting instructions to determine amount)
> coordinating solid (see cutting instructions to determine amount)
• 18-inch-wide tubular knit as indicated on pattern for binding
• Separating zipper as indicated in pattern
• Embroidery machine
• Machine embroidery design
• Threads:
> 1 spool of machine embroidery
> 2 or 3 cones of serger thread or contrasting spool thread for flat lock
> 4 cones of serger thread
• Fabric stabilizer
• Basic sewing supplies and equipment

Kwik Sew pattern No. 2536 was used for model project.

Pattern Preparation
• Since separating zippers cannot be adjusted with the method used here, be sure to adjust the length of the vest accordingly.
• Overlap seam lines of vest yoke and vest front to omit that seam. Mark a cutting line 1½ inches below the armhole.
• Cut pattern apart on marked line and add a ¼-inch seam allowance to both edges.
• Cut off the cut-on pocket on lower fronts by extending the side seams to make the sides straight.

Cutting
From print fleece fabric:
• Use pattern to cut back, lower fronts, collar and pockets. Transfer markings.

From solid fleece fabric:
• Use pattern to cut upper fronts. Transfer markings.

From tubular rib knit:
• Cut into 1½-inch-wide strips for binding.

Embroidery
Layer stabilizer and fleece in embroidery hoop. Refer to embroidery machine owner's manual to embroider design in desired location on upper yoke.

Assembly

Use a wide 2- or 3-thread flatlock with a short stitch length, unless otherwise stated. Use polyester or poly/cotton blend thread. Press as you sew.

1. Clip to dots on side seam of each lower front. Serge with a 3- or 4-thread overlock to edge finish, fold under and topstitch in place, starting and stopping even with dots to make the pocket opening.

2. Set serger for 2- or 3-thread flatlock. Shorten stitch length for better coverage. With wrong sides together, serge upper and lower fronts together. Pull layers open along seam to lay flat. Serge shoulder seams together. Pull layers open along seam to lay flat. ***Optional:*** *To create a ready-to-wear look, straight stitch down the center of the flatlock seam.*

3. Fold over pocket extension on each side of back along dots so wrong sides are together. Pin fronts and back with wrong sides together, matching raw edges (Figure 1). ***Note:*** *Fold of pocket will show under the front pocket opening.*

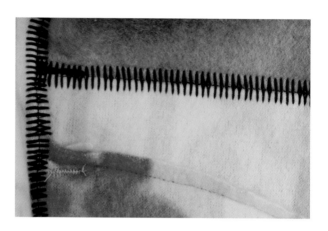

4. Flatlock side seams, catching back fold of each pocket without catching the folded front pocket opening. Fold pockets to fronts and topstitch in place. Work a bar tack at the top and bottom of opening on each pocket.

5. Reset serger to 4-thread overlock set for widest stitch width. Recheck vest length with zipper length and mark bottom of vest. Adjust as needed.

6. Position edge of binding strip along right side of bottom vest for hem (Figure 2). Serge binding to vest by running edge of ribbing just to blade and holding ribbing taut to vest. ***Note:*** *Do not stretch binding too much or it will make vest cup in at hem and armholes.*

Figure 1

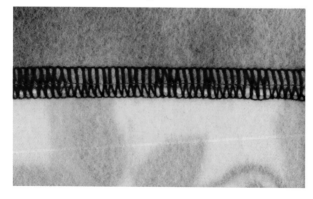

Figure 2   **Figure 3**

7. Fold binding to wrong side and stitch in the ditch. Trim excess binding on wrong side close to stitching (Figure 3).

8. Measure finished circumference of each armhole. Stretch binding slightly and cut to this length. On sewing machine, stitch ends of ribbing right sides together using a scant ¼-inch seam allowance.

9. Position edge of binding at finished edge of armhole on right side of vest. Adjust to fit armhole and serge, running edges of binding and fleece along the blade. Turn ribbing to wrong side. Stitch in the ditch and trim as for bottom binding.

10. With right sides together, match edge of zipper tape to front edge of vest. Use zipper foot on sewing machine to straight stitch close to teeth. Repeat to attach remaining side of zipper to opposite front edge.

11. Serge collar pieces right sides together along long seam line. Wrap corners (Figure 4) and serge short edges. Turn right side out.

Figure 4

12. With right sides together, serge outer collar to neck edge. Turn collar to inside, overlapping serged seam. Stitch in the ditch catching inside collar to finish inside seam. Trim excess fleece close to stitching.

13. Topstitch zipper and collar edges. **§**

Source: Pattern No. 2536 from Kwik Sew Pattern Co. Inc.

Coverstitch: More Than Hems
Create triple-coverstitch lace using the serger and turn a classic-style jacket into a one of-a-kind fashion.

By Cheryl Stranges

Finished size
Your size

Materials
• Purchased jacket pattern with yoke neckline*
• Linen fabric as indicated on pattern for view B
    (less pocket flaps)
• Water-soluble stabilizer
• Tear-away stabilizer
• Fusible interfacing as indicated on pattern
• Embellishments:
    40 percent wool/30 percent kid mohair/20
        percent silk/10 percent nylon blend yarn
    Angelina fiber
    silk ribbon flowers
    heat-set pearls and applicator tool
• 1-inch decorative button
• 4 (15mm) snap fasteners
• Embroidery machine with 3-D or 4-D and flower
    embroidery designs*
• Threads:
    2 spools 30- or 40-weight rayon embroidery
        or multicolored cotton
    60-weight bobbin
    4 cones polyester to match fabric
    3 (500-yard) spools multicolored cotton

• Felting machine
• Basic sewing supplies and equipment

Kwik Sew pattern no. 3577 ; Husqvarna Viking Embroidery No. 181 Textures & Techniques with M'Liss by M'Liss Rae Hawley was used for model project.

Triple Coverstitch Lace
1. Refer to owner's manual to set serger for triple coverstitch with multicolored cotton thread in needles and two cones polyester thread in coverstitch looper at the same time. **Note:** *Place one spool on the serger spool pin and the other on a thread stand on the table.*

2. Cut two pieces water-soluble stabilizer and one piece of tear-away stabilizer large enough to accommodate front and back neck band pattern pieces twice.

3. Lightly spray one side of one piece of water-soluble stabilizer with temporary spray adhesive. Lay strands of yarn across stabilizer to cover (Figure 1).

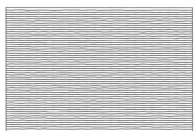

Figure 1

4. Arrange strands of Angelina fibers over yarn as desired. Lightly spray one side of second piece of water-soluble stabilizer and carefully place over fibers.

5. Place sandwich under serger needles so that needle thread will rest on top of the fabric. Serge across sandwiched layers in same direction as yarn, beginning at one side and stitching across to opposite side, cover from top to bottom, being sure you catch each last row of coverstitch with the next row. Continue stitching in this manner to completely cover stabilizer (Figure 2).

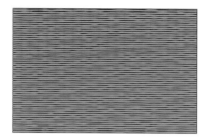

Figure 2

6. Layer tear-away stabilizer and serged-fiber sandwich; straight-stitch around layers on sewing machine. Follow manufacturer's instructions to remove water-soluble stabilizer. Hang to dry. When completely dry, remove tear-away stabilizer.

Cutting
From fabric:
• Cut jacket fronts, jacket back, front tabs, sleeves, back neck band facing and front neck band facings as indicated in pattern instructions.

From coverstitch lace:
• Use patterns to cut one back neck band and two front neck bands as indicated in pattern instructions.

Tips & Techniques

Knit tricot fusible interfacing is soft and does not change the hand of the fabric. It can be used on all different types of fabric, including wovens.

Assembly
Use 3- or 4-thread overlock with ¼-inch wide seam and medium stitch length, unless otherwise stated. Press as you sew.

1. Mark general location of embroidery on jacket back. Hoop jacket back with tear-away stabilizer. Embroider design. Remove from hoop and remove stabilizer following manufacturer's instructions.

2. Follow pattern steps 2–5 using serger or sewing machine using ⅝-inch seam allowance, trimming fabric as needed on serger.

3. Apply interfacing to front tabs as instructed in pattern. Draw a guideline down right side of right tab and spray-baste yarn in place in a random vining pattern. Using felting machine, felt yarn in place (Figure 3).

Figure 3

4. Continue with pattern instructions 7 and 8 to assemble neck band.

5. Complete construction of jacket as instructed in pattern steps 9–11, replacing buttonholes with hidden snaps behind embellished front tab.

6. Randomly hand-stitch ribbon flowers on neckband and down embellished front tab. Apply heat-set pearls to centers of flowers. **§**

Sources: Pattern No. 3577 from Kwik Sew Pattern Co. Inc.; thread from Sulky of America; ER10 Embellishing machine, Designer Diamond embroidery/sewing machine and Huskylock 936 serger from Husqvarna Viking Sewing Machine Co.

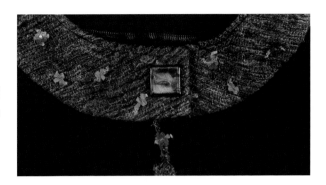

Serge a Simple Jacket
Naturally renewable silk and cotton fabrics complement one another, and used together, create a long–wearing garment.

By Cheryl Stranges

Finished size
Your size

Materials
- Kwik Sew jacket pattern No. 3531
- 54-inch-wide silk dupioni:
     1½ yards main color
     ¼ yard contrasting color for collar
- 3 yards 44/45-inch-wide lining fabric
- 2 yards 44/45-inch-wide 100 percent cotton print
- ¼ yard 44/45-inch-wide organza
- 36 x 44 inches 100 percent cotton batting
- ½ yard tear-away stabilizer
- 4 yards 24-inch-wide tricot fusible interfacing
- 11–12 heat-set brass stud embellishments
- Heat-set applicator tool
- Large fashion button
- Angelina fiber for embellishment
- 15mm snap
- Threads:
     4 cones serger
     30- and 40-weight rayon embroidery
     60-weight polyester bobbin
     100 percent cotton
     12-weight multicolored cotton
- Embroidery machine with 3-D or 4-D program
- Machine embroidery design
- Basic sewing supplies and equipment

Notes: *Serge around edges of cotton fabric (to prevent raveling) and wash to preshrink.*

To preshrink silk slightly, press using a press cloth and moderate steam. Silk Dupioni can also be hand-washed and hung to dry.

Cutting
From main color silk dupioni:
- Cut view A jacket fronts and back as indicated in pattern instructions.

From contrasting color silk dupioni:
- Cut two jacket collars as indicated in pattern instructions.

From cotton print:
- Cut view A jacket front and back facings as indicated in pattern instructions.
- Cut two rectangles slightly larger than needed for cutting each sleeve.

From lining fabric:
- Cut view A jacket fronts and back as indicated in pattern instructions.
- Cut two rectangles slightly larger than needed for cutting each sleeve.

From tricot fusible interfacing:
- Cut view A jacket front facing, back facing, front and back.
- Cut two collars.

From batting:
- Cut two rectangles slightly larger than needed for each sleeve.

Assembly

Use a 4-thread overlock with ¼-inch-wide seam and medium stitch length unless otherwise stated. Do not trim the fabric, only serge to edge finish. Use polyester or poly/cotton serger thread. Use ⅝-inch seam allowance on your sewing machine, unless otherwise stated.

1. Fuse interfacing to wrong sides of corresponding fabric pieces. Spray-baste lining pieces onto interfacing.

2. Using a 4-thread overlock, stitch around edges of each silk, lining and cotton pattern piece to prevent frayed edges.

3. Follow step 2 and 3 of pattern instructions.

4. Refer to your owner's manual to adjust serger for chain stitch. Change thread to 12-weight multicolored cotton and chain-stitch to embellish outer collar (Figure 1). **Note:** *Remember to chain-stitch on the wrong side of the collar.* Sew collar to jacket, following step 4 of pattern.

Figure 1

5. Sew front facings to back facing, right sides together, at shoulder seams. Trim seam allowances and press open.

6. Follow steps 6, 7, 8 and 9 of pattern.

7. Tear a 5- to 8-inch-wide strip of cotton print the width of the jacket back. Repeat with organza. Spray-baste cotton strip wrong side down on right side of silk jacket back. Arrange Angelina fibers over cotton strip, then spray-baste organza strip over the cotton strip.

8. Using straight stitch on the sewing machine, stitch along both long edges and across sleeve area. Using a decorative serpentine stitch and multicolor cotton, sew two or three rows across the layered strip. Use a press cloth to fuse Angelina fiber following manufacturer's instructions.

9. Hoop stabilizer, then spray-baste jacket back onto hoop for embroidery. Using 40-weight rayon embroidery thread and 60-weight bobbin thread, embroider selected design. Remove from hoop and tear away stabilizer.

10. Layer the lining, batting and cotton sleeve rectangles with cotton on top, right side up. Spray-baste layers together. Thread sewing machine with decorative thread and set for free-motion sewing. Quilt layers together following cotton print designs. When completed, cut out sleeves. Finish edges to prevent fraying.

11. Finish constructing jacket as instructed in pattern steps 10–13.

12. To embellish, lightly wrap multicolored cotton thread around two fingers approximately 20 times. Remove from fingers and twist loops in center (Figure 2). Tack to jacket front. Repeat to make 11 or 12 thread loops scattered over jacket front.

Figure 2

13. Sew fashion button to jacket right front as shown. Sew snap under button and on left front for closure.

14. Following manufacturer's instructions, attach a heat-set brass stud in the center of each twisted loop. §

Sources: Designer Diamond embroidery machine and Sparklers #138 embroidery design from Husqvarna Viking Sewing Machine Co.; jacket pattern #3531 from Kwik Sew Pattern Co. Inc.

Jeweled Batik Jacket
Create a fun and fashionable jacket with serged details on the inside and outside.

By Marianne Guy

Finished size
Your size

Materials
• Pattern for semifitted, dart-free, lined jacket with curved hemline*
• 44/45-inch-wide cotton batik fabric:
> 2 yards for outer jacket
> 2 yards coordinating print for lining
• 2½ yards soft fusible batting
• 4mm–5mm heat-set crystals and applicator wand
• ¼-inch-wide satin ribbon to contrast with decorative threads
• Threads:
> Decorative for embellishing (12-weight cotton, rayon, etc.) for loopers
> 2 cones serger to match decorative threads for needle(s)
• 2 beaded tassels (from home dec department)
• Basic sewing supplies and equipment

Model project was made using The Pop Top Jacket pattern No. 108 by Jennifer Amor.

Cutting
From outer jacket fabric:
• Follow pattern instructions to cut out jacket fronts, back and sleeves.

• Cut one 1¼ x 5-inch strip for tassel loops.

From coordinating print for lining:
• Follow pattern instructions to cut out jacket fronts, back and sleeves.

From soft fusible batting:
• Follow pattern instructions to cut out jacket fronts, back and sleeves.

Assembly
Use a 4-thread overlock for edge finishing and seaming, with a ¼-inch wide seam and medium stitch length. Use polyester or poly/cotton blend thread. Refer to your owner's manual for serger set up for chain stitch and cover stitch. Use decorative thread in the loopers and serger thread (or the same thread as used for edge finishing and seaming) in the needles. Press as you sew.

1. Fuse soft batting pieces to jacket pieces following manufacturer's instructions.

2. Adjust your serger to cover stitch; followed by the chain stitch. Using both stitches in a random pattern, embellish the jacket by meandering around the front, back and sleeve pieces. Place jacket pieces wrong sides up to embellish with the looper thread, as well as chain-stitching on the right side for more detail.

3. Weave ribbon through looper side of cover stitches on right side of jacket. Place a dab of seam sealant at beginning and end of each cover stitch and/or chain stitch.

4. Adjust serger to 4-thread overlock. Serge jacket shoulder and side seams, trimming seams to ¼-inch wide. Set sleeves with a sewing machine using a ⅝-inch seam allowance, then finish and trim allowance to ¼-inch using the serger.

5. Assemble lining in same manner as jacket.

6. Follow pattern instructions for completing jacket assembly.

7. Fold strip for tassel loops in half lengthwise. Sew long edges together using a ¼-inch seam allowance. Turn right side out. Press with seam in center of one side. Cut in half to make two loops.

8. Slip a beaded tassel onto each loop, then turn raw ends under and stitch together. Sew loops onto sleeves.

9. Apply heat-set crystals randomly to jacket. §

Source: The Pop Top Jacket pattern No. 108 by Jennifer Amor.

Around the House

Creating a perfect home is little more than having the right home decor at the right time. You'll love to update your home with these quick home remakes.

Button Valance

Hang this sunny valance at your window to make even gloomy days look bright. Accent buttons reveal peekaboo pleats that give this simple treatment added flair.

By Carol Zentgraf

Finished size
40½ x 14 inches

Materials
• 44/45-inch-wide cotton fabric:
  ½ yard decorative print (A)
  ⅝ yards contrasting print (B)
• Cover button forms:
  2 (1⅛-inch)
  4 (⅝-inch)
• Permanent fabric adhesive
• 3 or 4 cones serger thread
• Basic sewing supplies and equipment

Cutting
From (A) fabric:
• Cut three 14½ x 14-inch rectangles for valance.

From (B) fabric:
• Cut one 42 x 5-inch strip for rod pocket.
• Cut two 14½ x 14-inch rectangles for pleats.

Assembly
Use 3- or 4-thread overlock with ¼-inch-wide seam and medium stitch length, unless otherwise stated. Use polyester or poly/cotton blend thread. Press as you sew.

1. Serge a pleat panel to each 14-inch edge of one valance panel. Serge the two remaining valance panels to the remaining 14-inch edges of the pleat panels. Press seams toward valance panels (Figure 1).

Figure 1

2. Serge side and lower edges of assembled panels to finish. Press sides under ½ inch; topstitch in place. Press lower edge under 1 inch; topstitch in place.

3. Mark center of upper and lower edges of each pleat panel. Press along seam lines and bring folded edges to center marks, leaving a ⅛-inch space between folded edges (Figure 2). Press pleats in place. Baste upper edges together.

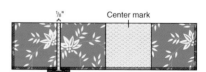

Figure 2

4. Press under ½ inch on one long edge of rod pocket strip. Center the remaining long edge on upper edge of valance, right sides together. Serge rod pocket

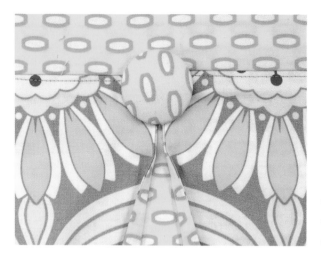

to pleated panel taking care that basted pleats are stitched in the serging. Press seam toward rod pocket. Serge short ends of rod pocket, and press under short edges to match ends of valance.

5. Fold rod pocket to back of valance with pressed-under back edge ¼ inch lower than the front edge. Press upper edge and topstitch pressed-under edge in place.

6. Follow manufacturer's instructions to cover 1⅛-inch cover button forms with scraps of (B) fabric, and ⅝-inch cover button forms with scraps of (A) fabric.

7. Sew large buttons to tops of pleats. Glue edges of pleats to pleat back ½ inch below each button (Figure 3). Let dry.

Figure 3

8. Turn bottom of each pleat out 1½ inches and press pleats open. Tack in place by sewing ⅝-inch buttons to pressed-back corners through all layers. §

Sources: Fabric from Westminster Fibers; covered button forms from Prym Consumer USA; Fabri-Tac permanent fabric adhesive from Beacon Adhesives.

Sizing Matters

Adjusting the window valance for various sizes of windows is simple.

1. Measure the desired window's width. Be sure to include additional coverage on each side. Add 2 inches to the desired width and divide by 3. This will give you the width of the three panels to be cut from fabric A.

2. Cut 2 panels from fabric B the same size as in step 1 above.

3. Finally, adjust the strip for the rod pocket by the initial desired width and add 1 inch for finishing on short ends of pocket.

Fly-Away Drapery

Customize these simple-to-serge drapes to add a fanciful touch to any size window!

By Carol Zentgraf

Finished size
Custom

Materials
• 44/45-inch-wide cotton fabric:
   decorative print for drapery panel
     and ties (A)
   coordinating print for valance (B)
• Scallop ruler with 9-inch-long scallops
• Drapery rod
• 3 or 4 cones serger thread
• Basic sewing supplies and equipment

Determine Yardage
1. Mount drapery rod 2–4 inches above the window.

2. Measure from 1 inch below the rod to the desired length for the draperies to determine the finished length of each drapery panel. Add 4 inches for hem allowance and ½ inch for an upper-edge seam allowance to determine the cut length of the panel.

3. Design uses two panels on a window. Finished width of both panels should be 1½ times the window width or more, depending on desired fullness. Add 2 inches to finished width measurement to determine

cut width. ***Note:*** *A fuller drape or larger window may require extra panel lengths or wider fabric to achieve the desired width.*

Cutting
From (A) fabric:
• Cut two panels each the determined cut width by cut length.
• Cut 28 strips each 2 x 12 inches for ties.

From (B) fabric:
• Cut four panels for valance each 16 inches by the determined cut width. Place two valance panels right

sides together with edges matching. Mark the center of the lower edge. Align the center of the scallop ruler with the center mark and draw a scallop line across the lower edge of the valance. Cut along line through both layers and pin layers together. Repeat with remaining valance panels.

Assembly

Use 3- or 4-thread overlock with ¼-inch-wide seam and medium stitch length, unless otherwise stated. Use polyester or poly/cotton blend thread. Press as you sew.

1. With wrong sides together, serge short edges of valance together. Turn lower edge of serged seam to lining side of valance, and straight stitch valance panels together along scallop edges using a ¼-inch seam allowance. Prior to stitching last scallop, turn serged seam to lining side of valance, and catch in the straight stitch. **Note:** *Turning and catching the serging in the seam gives a squared corner point.* Trim scalloped edge and clip inward points of scallops to stitching line. Turn valance right side out and press. Serge upper edges together.

2. Fold each tie strip in half lengthwise with right sides together. Serge long sides together and serge one short side. Turn strips right side out and position seam in back center. Press. Stack strips into 14 pairs with raw ends even and seams to the back. Serge raw ends of each pair together.

3. Serge long edges of each panel to finish. Press long edges to wrong side for a 1-inch hem. Beginning 2 inches from upper edge of each panel, topstitch hems in place.

4. Place panel wrong side up on work surface. Open unstitched side hems. Pin serged end of a pair of ties to upper edge of panel close to each fold. Pin another pair of ties to center of top edge. Evenly space and pin remaining pairs of ties across top edge of panel (Figure 1). Repeat with second panel. Baste ties to panel edge.

Figure 1

5. With side hems of panel still open, pin top edge of valance to wrong side of panel top edge with ends of valance even with fold lines of panel side hems. Serge across top edge. Finish topstitching side hems in place. Repeat with second panel.

6. Press seam toward panel. Topstitch through all layers ¼ inch from top edge of each panel.

7. Press under 2 inches at lower edge of each panel. Press under 2 inches again to make a 2-inch double hem. Topstitch in place. §

Sources: Fabric from Westminster Fibers; scallop ruler from June Tailor.

Jelly Roll Valance Go shabby chic, funky, retro or modern—jelly roll collections make it easy to coordinate fabrics to suit your style!

By Pamela Hastings

Finished size

44 x 11½ inches

Materials

- Jelly roll fabric collection
- 13 (¾-inch) grommets and grommet setting tool
- ½ yard fusible interfacing
- 6 yards ⅜-inch-wide grosgrain ribbon
- ⅝-inch-diameter curtain rod
- 3 or 4 cones serger thread
- Basic sewing supplies and equipment

Note: *For longer or shorter valance, increase or decrease the number of strips and adjust lengths of top-band strips accordingly.*

Cutting

From jelly roll fabric:

- Cut six 15-inch-long strips from three jelly roll strips for top band.

From fusible interfacing:

- Cut six 15 x 2¼-inch strips for top band.

From ribbon:

- Cut 13 (16-inch) lengths for attaching valance to rod.

Assembly

Use 3- or 4-thread overlock with ¼-inch-wide seam and medium stitch length, unless otherwise stated. Use polyester or poly/cotton blend thread. Press as you sew.

1. Fuse interfacing to wrong sides of top-band strips with interfacing even with one long (bottom) edge and both ends of top band strip. Serge together short edges of three top-band strips (Figure 1). Repeat with three remaining top-band strips.

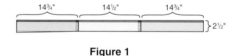

Figure 1

2. With right sides together and raw edges even, serge top-band strips together across top edge. Fold top band with wrong sides together to make 44½ x 2¼-inch top band.

3. Select 11 jelly roll strips and arrange in desired order side by side. Serge strips right sides together across long edges.

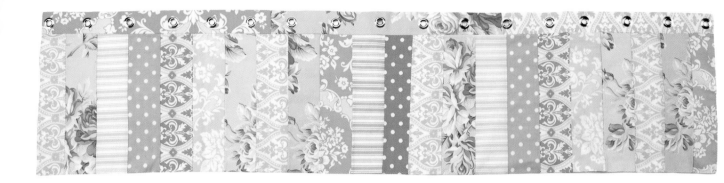

4. Cut serged unit in half to make two 20-inch-long units (Figure 2). With right sides together, serge units together across a 20-inch edge to make one 22-strip-wide valance unit.

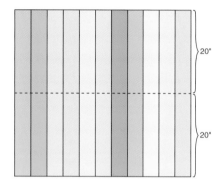

20"

20"

Figure 2

5. With right sides together and raw edges even, serge one bottom edge of top band to one edge of valance unit. Serge remaining bottom edge of top band to opposite edge of valance unit making a tube (Figure 3).

Figure 3

6. With right sides still together, fold valance in half, with top band positioned along the upper edge, evenly divided between front and back. Trim short edges of top band even with edges of valance unit,

if necessary. Pin sides of valance, matching band seam lines (Figure 4).

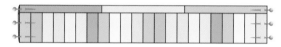

Figure 4

7. Serge edges of one side together. Serge edges of remaining side, leaving an opening for turning. Turn right side out. Press under opening seam allowance. Hand-stitch opening closed.

8. Following manufacturer's instructions, attach a grommet close to each end of top band. Attach remaining grommets evenly spaced between end grommets (approximately 2 inches apart).

9. Insert lengths of ribbon through grommets and tie around rod. §

Source: Fabric from Freespirit.

Quick & Easy Pillow Cover

You'll love this simple-to-serge pillow cover with a hidden seam casing. The secret lies in how the fabric is folded.

By Sue Greene-Baker

Finished size

22½ x 33 inches

Materials

• Lightweight cotton fabric:

    27 x 45-inch rectangle for pillowcase

    12 x 45-inch rectangle for hem/band

    2½ x 45-inch strip for trim insert

• 3 or 4 cones serger thread

• Basic sewing supplies and equipment

Assembly

Use a 3- or 4-thread overlock with a ¼-inch-wide seam and medium stitch length, unless otherwise stated. Use polyester or poly/cotton thread. Press as you sew.

1. Press 2½-inch trim strip in half lengthwise with wrong sides together.

2. Lay hem/band fabric on flat surface in a single layer, right side up.

3. Lay pillowcase fabric in a single layer on top of the hem/band fabric, right side up, matching top long raw edges.

Tips & Techniques

• *Smooth out the tail chain and lay it on the serger seam. Stitch over it using a close zigzag stitch, securing it to the seam allowance. Clip excess tail chain and sewing threads to make a neat ending.*

• *For more variation, layer gathered lace between the hem/band and the trim inset; substitute decorative cord or other trim; add a scalloped edge to the hem/band.*

4. Lay pressed trim on top of pillowcase fabric, matching cut edges. Pin all layers together (Figure 1).

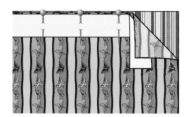

Figure 1

5. Roll up the pillowcase fabric to an inch or two below the trim insert (Figure 2).

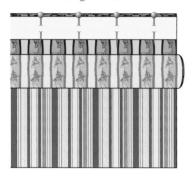

Figure 2

6. Wrap the bottom edge of the hem/band fabric over the top of the rolled-up pillowcase fabric, enclosing it inside the hem/band (Figure 3). Pin the lower edge of the hem/band to the other pinned fabrics. **Note:** *The hem/band will be wrapped completely around the pillowcase and trim fabrics. There will be five layers of fabric pinned together.*

Figure 3

7. Rotate the serger hand wheel to bring the needles to the highest position and open the knife blades. Raise the presser foot and insert the edges of the fabrics in front of the open knife blades. Lower the foot and stitch across the 45-inch pinned edge, removing pins as you stitch and trimming fabric edges even.

8. Turn pillowcase right side out through one open end. Press turned pillowcase to set the trim, seam and edge of the band.

9. Fold right sides together again across the 45-inch width to make a 22½ x 33-inch pillowcase. Pin the side seam, matching edges of hem/band and trim strip. Serge the side seam, trimming a scant ⅛ inch off the seam. Press seam to one side.

10. Starting at the serged side seam edge, serge the end of the pillowcase closed. Fold ends to press seam allowance to one side, being careful not to press a crease in the folds of the triangle (Figure 4). **Note:** *This seam must be pressed in two steps.* Turn right side out and press. §

Figure 4

More Pillow Talk

For a quick alternative, substitute a wide eyelet lace trim for the hem/band instead of folded fabric. The finished seam will not be enclosed, but the serger makes such a nice finish, it won't matter.

1. Cut fabrics as instructed for pillowcase. Cut eyelet lace approximately 6½ inches wide.

2. Press inset trim strip. Layer all three pieces, matching raw edges. Pin together. Serge across top raw edges.

3. Finish side and end seams.

Picture-Perfect Place Setting
Create quick-and-easy "frames" in neutral fabric, and then add inserts to accent every holiday and special occasion!

By Sue Greene-Baker

Finished size
18 x 13 inches

Materials
• 44/45-inch-wide mediumweight woven fabric:
    ½ yard neutral solid
    ½ yard each two different prints
    1 yard fusible interfacing
• Thread:
    Decorative thread in upper looper such
      as pearl cotton or buttonhole twist
• 2 cones serger thread
• Basic sewing supplies and equipment

Cutting
From neutral mediumweight woven fabric:
• Cut one 20 x 15-inch rectangle for frame.

From each of two different prints:
• Cut one 17 x 12-inch rectangle for insert.

From fusible interfacing:
• Cut one 20 x 15-inch rectangle for frame.
• Cut two 17 x 12-inch rectangles for insert.

Assembly
Use a 3-thread overlock with a wide seam and decorative thread in upper looper and regular-weight serger thread in needle and lower looper. Adjust stitch length for a balanced satin-stitch edge.

1. Fuse interfacing to wrong side of neutral rectangle. Serge around all four edges.

2. Fold a 1½-inch hem to the wrong side on all four sides; press to crease (Figure 1). **Note:** *If using woolly nylon for decorative thread, avoid touching thread with the iron.*

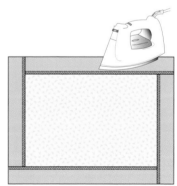

Figure 1

3. Open the hems and fold each corner diagonally at exactly where the crease lines meet. Press the fold to crease the fabric (Figure 2).

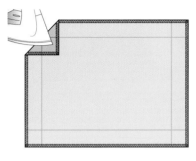

Figure 2

4. Fold place mat right sides together, forming a point at one corner (Figure 3). Serge from outside edge to corner point, exactly on the crease line to form the corner miter. Turn corner to the right side. Repeat for each remaining corner.

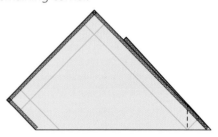

Figure 3

Serger Napkins From Sheets

1. Remove hems from the top and bottom of a twin-size sheet by clipping the fabric just below the top hem and just above the bottom hem and ripping off the hems (Figure 4).

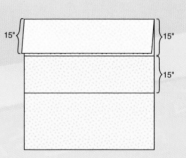

Figure 5

4. Fold fabric in the other direction and press a crease every 15 inches (Figure 6). If last crease is not an even 15 inches, rip off excess strip.

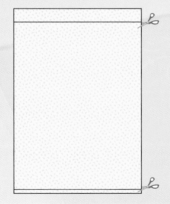

Figure 4

2. Fold the top edge of the sheet down 15 inches and press a crease.

3. Continue to fold and press the sheet every 15 inches until there are three rows (Figure 5). Rip the fabric on the last crease to make fabric that measures the full width and 45 inches long.

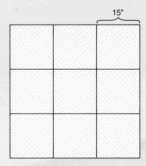

Figure 6

5. Serge fabric, letting the serger knife cut on the fold to serge the edge while cutting them out at the same time!

5. Turn frame right side out and press miters and folded edges into a sharp edge.

6. Fuse interfacing to the wrong side of each 17 x 12-inch rectangle. Pin rectangles with wrong sides together and serge together around edges.

7. Slip insert into frame to display desired side. §

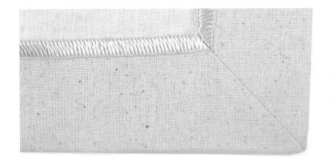

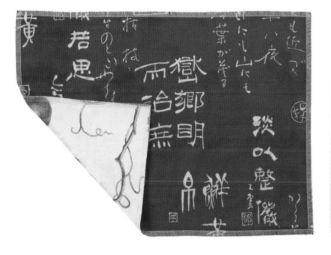

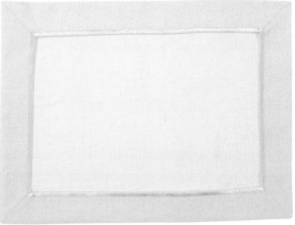

Reversible Batik Topper

Use a flip 'n stitch method to serge a reversible table topper quickly and easily.

By Carolyn Vagts

Finished size

28 x 28 inches

Materials

• 44/45-inch-wide batik fabric:
> ⅓ yard light
> ⅝ yard dark
> ¾ yard medium
> ⅞ yard coordinating print
• Crib-size batting
• 3 or 4 cones serger thread
• Basic sewing supplies and equipment

Cutting

From light batik fabric:

• Cut two 12 x 12-inch squares for center.

From dark batik fabric:

• Cut two 19 x 19-inch squares. Cut from corner to corner twice to make four triangles from each square.

From medium batik fabric:

• Cut six 2-inch strips the width of the fabric for sashing.
• Cut four 2½-inch strips the width of the fabric for binding.

From coordinating print batik fabric:

• Cut six 5-inch strips the width of the fabric for outer border.

From batting:

• Cut one 12 x 12-inch square for center.
• Cut one 19 x 19-inch square. Cut from corner to corner twice to make four triangles from each square.
• Cut two 2 x 18-inch strips and two 2 x 20-inch strips for sashing.
• Cut two 5 x 20-inch strips and two 5 x 30-inch strips for outer border.

Assembly

Use 3- or 4-thread overlock with ¼-inch-wide seam and medium stitch length, unless otherwise stated. Use polyester or poly/cotton blend thread. Press as you sew.

Note: *Cut sashing and border strips slightly longer than needed, then trim to length after you have squared up and serged piece.*

1. Sandwich batting center square between wrong sides of fabric center squares with raw edges even. Serge around edges. Free motion stitch or embroider center square as desired.

2. Place one batting triangle on work surface. Place one fabric triangle right side up over batting triangle with all edges even. Place one 12-inch edge of square on long edge of triangles, then another fabric triangle over the square, making sure all pieces are lined up

and centered (Figure 1). **Note:** *Triangle pieces will be longer than square.* Serge edges together. Repeat on opposite side of square and trim to size.

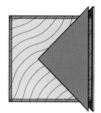

Figure 1

3. Open triangles so right sides are all facing out. Press and make sure both sides are equal. If not, trim. Serge unfinished edges of triangles (Figure 2). **Note:** *The points of the triangles will be longer than the square.*

Figure 2

4. Repeat step 2 to attach triangles to remaining sides of center square (Figure 3). Open triangles so right sides are all facing out and serge outer raw edges (Figure 4).

Figure 3

Figure 4

5. Using same layering order, pin the top and bottom sashing strips in place and serge. Open up strips so right sides are all facing out and serged edges are

inside. Press, making sure sashing strips are the same width. Trim if needed. Serge unfinished edges (Figure 5). Attach sashing to sides in same manner as for top and bottom. Serge to edge finish.

Figure 5

6. Repeat step 5 to add outer border strips (Figure 6).

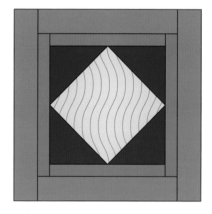

Figure 6

7. Join binding strips to make one long strip. Fold in half lengthwise and press. Unfold one end and trim it in a 45-degree angle. Turn angled edge under ½ inch. Refold and press (Figure 7).

Figure 7

8. Using a ¼-inch seam allowance and straight stitch, begin in center of one side and sew binding strip with raw edges matching to front side of topper. Stop stitching ¼ inch from first corner. Angle sewing direction to a 45-degree angle and sew off to corner point (Figure 8).

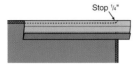

Figure 8

9. Flip binding up away from topper (Figure 9), then fold it back into place along the next edge to be stitched (Figure 10). Continue stitching around topper, working each corner in the same manner.

Figure 10

10. Trim end of binding so it can be tucked inside the end of beginning end. Finish stitching seam.

11. Turn folded edge of binding over raw edges of topper and hand-stitch in place on back of topper. §

Figure 9

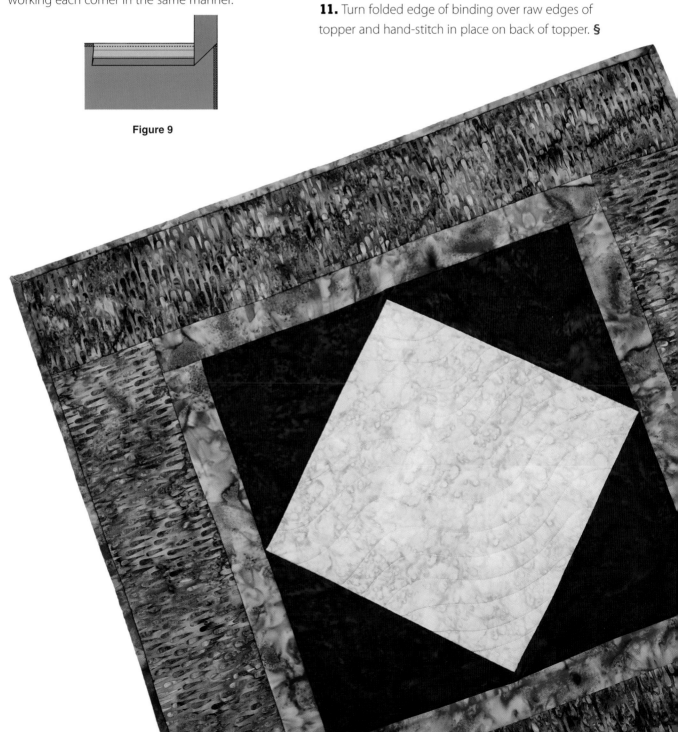

Scrappy Braid Place Mat
Quilting is as easy as one, two, three when you let your serger do all the work.

By Barbara Rezac

Finished size
Approximately 19 x 13 inches

Materials
• 44/45-inch lightweight woven fabric:
  ¼ yard background print
  ¼ yard border print
• Assorted scraps lightweight woven fabric
• 4 cones neutral serger thread
• Clear acrylic quilter's ruler
• 4 cones serger thread
• Basic sewing supplies and equipment

Cutting
From background print fabric:
• Cut three 2½-inch strips the width of the fabric for background strips.
• Cut one 1½ x 17-inch strip for sashing.

From border print fabric:
• Cut two 2½-inch strips the width of the fabric for borders.

From assorted scraps:
• Cut 26 (3½ x 1½-inch) strips for long scrappy pieces.
• Cut 26 (2½ x 1½-inch) strips for short scrappy pieces.

Assembly
Use a 4-thread overlock. Set stitch width to make an accurate ¼-inch-wide seam with a medium width. Use cotton thread in loopers and needles. Sew right sides together and press as you sew.

1. Place the end of a large scrappy piece on the edge of one background strip. Pin in place (Figure 1). Continue adding long scrappy pieces, leaving about ⅛ inch between them, until all 26 are pinned to the background strip. Serge, removing pins prior to serging.

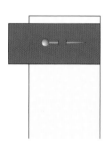

Figure 1

2. Repeat step 1 with short scrappy pieces.

3. Press pieces away from background strip with seam allowance toward scraps.

4. Line up ruler with edge of scrappy strip and cut strips apart using a rotary cutter (Figure 2). Trim both sides of attached background strips even with scrappy pieces.

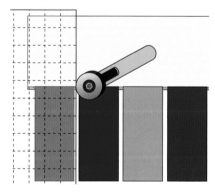

Figure 2

5. Arrange units in two rows: one with the 3½-inch pieces on the right and the other with the 3½-inch pieces on the left, creating a mirror image (Figure 3).

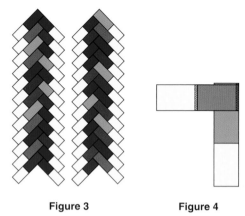

Figure 3   **Figure 4**

6. Working with the units in one row, serge the end of a 2½-inch strip to the side of a 3½-inch strip (Figure 4).

7. Serge the side of another 2½-inch strip across the end and side of the previously joined unit (Figures 5a and 5b).

a.   b.

Figure 5

8. Continue serging strips together until joined units measure 17½-inch-long. Repeat steps 6–8 with second row of units.

9. On both sides of each strip, measure ½ inch from corner of scrappy pieces. Align ruler with marks and trim with a rotary cutter (Figure 6).

Figure 6

10. Serge one edge of sashing strip to center edge of each scrappy strip to join.

11. Cut two border strips to fit across ends of place mat. Fold in half lengthwise with wrong sides together and serge raw edges to ends of place mat.

12. Measure length of place mat top and bottom edges and add ½ inch. Cut two border strips this length. Fold lengthwise with right sides together and serge across short ends. Turn right side out; press. Serge raw edges to top and bottom of place mat. Press. §

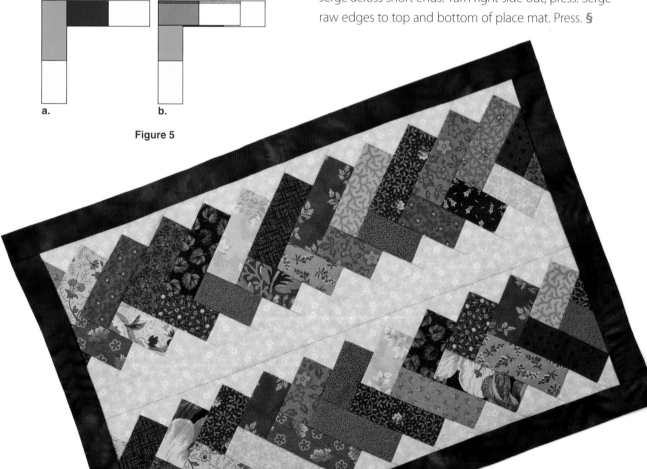

Elegant Embroidered Runner

Combine serging with machine embroidery to create this stylish table runner. Using plaid fabric gives the look of quilting with no piecing.

By Nancy Estep

Finished size

48 x 14 inches

Materials

- 54-inch-wide home decor fabric:
    - ¾ yard main color
    - ⅓ yard coordinating plaid
    - 5 x 28 inches coordinating solid color
- 3½ yards piping cord
- Threads:
    - Decorative machine embroidery threads to match plaid and solid fabrics
    - 3 or 4 cones serger thread
- Sewing machine with embroidery capability or purchased appliqués
- Machine embroidery designs
- Paper-backed fusible web
- Serger piping foot
- Basic sewing supplies and equipment

Cutting

From main-color fabric:

- Cut one 49 x 15-inch piece for back.
- Cut two 32½ x 3½-inch pieces for side borders.
- Cut four 2½ x 8½-inch pieces for center strips.

- Cut two 14½ x 9½-inch pieces for runner ends.
- Cut ends as shown in Figure 1.

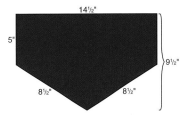

Figure 1

From coordinating plaid fabric:

- Cut six 4½ x 4½-inch squares for pieced blocks.
- Cut 1¼-inch-wide strips to equal 3½ yards when joined for piping cord cover.

From coordinating solid-color fabric:

- Cut six 4½ x 4½-inch squares for pieced blocks.

Appliqués

1. Use template (page 126) to trace eight appliqués onto paper side of fusible web. Cut out just outside traced lines.

2. Fuse four onto wrong sides of solid-color fabric remnants and four onto wrong sides of plaid fabric remnants. Cut out on traced lines.

3. Referring to Figure 2, fuse two plaid appliqués in the corners of two solid block squares and two solid appliqués to two plaid block squares. Satin-stitch upper edge of each appliqué using matching thread. Set appliquéd blocks aside.

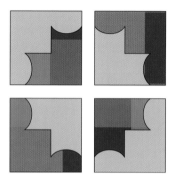

Figure 2

4. Position one plaid and one solid appliqué on center of straight edge of one runner end piece, overlapping seam allowances. Satin-stitch upper and center edges using matching thread for each appliqué. Set appliquéd runner ends aside.

Assembly

Use a 3- or 4-thread overlock with a ¼-inch-wide seam and medium stitch length unless otherwise stated. Use polyester or poly/cotton blend thread. Press as you sew.

1. Serge one plaid appliquéd square and one solid appliquéd square together with appliqués in center corners. Repeat with second set of appliquéd squares, alternating colors. Serge the two units together to make the center block (Figure 3).

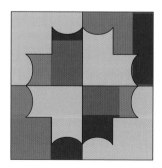

Figure 3

2. Serge one plaid square and one solid square together. Repeat with a second plaid and solid square. Serge the two units together, alternating colors to make a plain block. Serge remaining squares together in same manner to make third block.

3. Join blocks by serging a center strip to both edges of each block to form the center of the table runner.

4. Serge side borders to each side of runner center. Serge runner ends to each end of runner center.

5. Embellish appliqués with embroidery design of choice, or fuse purchased appliqués to blocks following manufacturers directions.

6. Place finished top on back piece. Cut back to fit top.

7. Use piping foot to serge raw edges of piping cord cover strip over piping cord. Serge piping around edge of runner top, butting ends of piping together and turning fabric under ¼ inch at the end and continuing stitching.

8. With right sides together, serge front and back together, leaving an opening for turning. Turn right side out and press. Fuse opening closed using paper-backed fusible web. **§**

Source: Steam-A-Seam 2 paper-backed fusible web from The Warm Company.

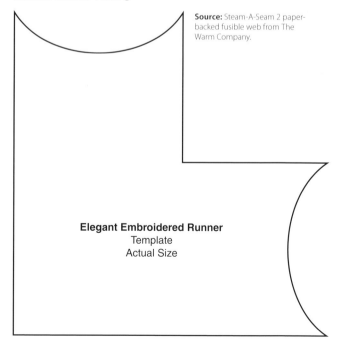

Elegant Embroidered Runner
Template
Actual Size

Heirloom Pillow Use your gathering foot, and rolled edge and flatlock stitches to create keepsake memories. Decorative thread and ribbon add the final touches.

By Sue Greene-Baker

Finished size
14 x 14 inches

Materials
• ¾ yard 44/45-inch-wide lightweight cotton fabric
• ⅞ yard 1½-inch-wide decorative lace
• ⅞ yard ⅜-inch-wide edging lace
• 2¾ yards ⅛-inch-wide satin ribbon
• 1⅝ yard 2¼-inch-wide gathered lace
• 14 x 14-inch pillow form
• Gathering foot
• 3 or 4 cones serger thread
• Basic sewing supplies and equipment

Cutting

From lightweight cotton fabric:
• Cut two 6½ x 14½-inch rectangles for pillow top.
• Cut two 10½ x 14½-inch rectangles for pillow back.
• Cut one 2¾-inch strip the width of the fabric for gathered insertion.
• Cut four 3¼-inch strips the width of the fabric for ruffle.

From insertion lace:
• Cut two 15-inch lengths.

From edging lace:
• Cut two 15-inch lengths.

From satin ribbon:
• Cut four 15-inch lengths to embellish pillow top.
• Cut four 10-inch lengths for bows at pillow corners.

Assembly
Use a 3- or 4-thread overlock with a ¼-inch-wide seam and medium stitch length, unless otherwise stated. Use polyester or poly/cotton blend thread. Press as you sew.

1. Serge ends of ruffle strips together. Finish one long edge with a rolled hem. Attach gathering foot to serger. Refer to owner's manual to gather opposite long edge. Set ruffle aside.

2. With gathering foot still attached, gather both edges of 2¾-inch strip for gathered insertion. Trim finished gathered piece to 14½ inches long.

3. On right side of pillow top unit, mark 1¼ inch. Measure and mark an additional 1½ inch (Figure 1). Fold fabric with wrong sides together, press along one mark from top to bottom. Repeat for second mark.

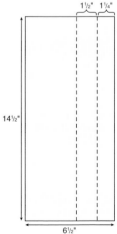

Figure 1

4. Refer to your owner's manual and adjust serger for flatlock serging. Position edging lace underneath folded edge of fabric fold. Place decorative lace on top of folded edge, and top with ribbon. Position stack with fabric fold and ribbon/lace edges flush against the cutting system. Taking care not to trim fabric or ribbon, or to catch the ribbon in the needle thread, serge over the ribbon to attach the ribbon and laces to fabric (Figure 2).

Figure 2

5. Repeat for second mark. Gently pull flat lock open. As needed, with finger tip, lightly run over stitching so laces and ribbon lay flat. Lightly press (Figure 3).

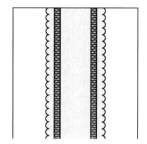

Figure 3

6. With wrong sides together, place edge of gathered insertion along long edge of 6½ x 14½-inch rectangle for pillow top. Serge; repeat for second side. Press serged seam to pillow top side. With sewing machine, straight-stitch edging lace over the serged seams on both sides.

7. Pin gathered lace around pillow top edge, then pin ruffle around edge of pillow over lace. Trim to fit and serge short ends of lace and ruffle together.

8. Sew a double ¼-inch hem in one long edge of each pillow back rectangle. Pin backs to pillow front, over ruffle, overlapping hemmed edges at center.

9. Serge all layers together, removing pins as you sew. Turn right side out. Press.

10. Hand-tack a 10-inch ribbon at each corner and tie in a bow. Insert pillow form in back. §

Polka Dot Tuffet
Not even a spider could get Miss Muffet off this tuffet! Select fabric and trim to make it fun and festive, or use fabrics that suit your decor.

By Carol Zentgraf

Finished size

Approximately 21 inches in diameter x 11 inches tall

Materials

• 44/45-inch-wide cotton fabric:
    1½ yards multicolored polka dot
    ⅛ yard coordinating pin dot
• 5 x 5-inch scrap contrasting pin dot cotton fabric
• 2 (22 x 22-inch) squares 4-inch-thick upholstery foam alternative
• 1¾ yards each two chenille ball fringe with decorative headers to match polka dot fabric
• 18-inch-diameter ¾-inch-thick wood circle
• 4 (5-inch) tall fencepost finials
• 3-inch cover button form
• 2-hole button at least 1 inch in diameter
• 12-inch-long upholstery needle
• Waxed button thread
• Sharp skewer
• Sharp heavy-duty scissors
• Medium-tip permanent marker

• Drill with ¼-inch bit
• Heavy-duty staple gun and staples
• Acrylic paint:
    white
    color to match fabric
• Flat paintbrush
• Clear plastic
• Permanent fabric adhesive
• 3 or 4 cones serger thread
• Basic sewing supplies and equipment

Foundation Structure

1. Mark the center of the wood circle. Draw two perpendicular lines across the board through the center, dividing the circle in fourths.

2. Measure the distance from the edge of the fencepost finial to the screw. Use this measurement to make a mark for the screw hole at the end of each drawn line on the board.

3. Drill screw holes for attaching finials, and another hole in the center of the board. Attach finials for legs.

4. Base-coat legs with white acrylic paint; let dry. Apply second coat in color to match fabric. Let dry.

5. Use a marker to trace the wood circle on one square of upholstery foam alternative. Draw a line 1½ inches from traced line to make a 21-inch-diameter circle. Cut out using heavy-duty scissors, cutting through the foam in layers from the top down. Glue the foam circle to the center of the remaining square of upholstery foam alternative and cut out a second circle.

6. Glue the board to the center of the foam circles; let dry. Turn foam side up. Mark circle center. Cutting gradually, use the scissors to shape the foam into a rounded shape (Figure 1).

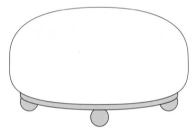

Figure 1

7. Place tuffet on its side. Insert the skewer through the center hole in the board and the center of the foam to create a channel for tufting.

8. Using center hole as a guide, draw lines across the foam and down the sides to divide surface into six equal wedges. Place plastic over one wedge section and trace lines to create a pattern (Figure 2).

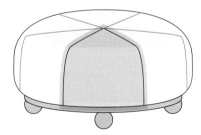

Figure 2

Cutting

From polka dot fabric:
- Use wedge pattern to cut six wedges, adding ¼ inch to side edges for seam allowances.

From coordinating pin dot fabric:
- Cut a 2 x 44-inch strip for center ruffle.

Assembly

Use 3- or 4-thread overlock with ¼-inch-wide seam and medium stitch length, unless otherwise stated. Use polyester or poly/cotton blend thread. Press as you sew.

1. Serge edges of fabric wedges together with right sides facing.

2. Center fabric over foam. Staple one edge to edge of board above one leg. Pull taut and staple the opposite edge to board above opposite leg. Repeat halfway between these points. Continue stapling in this manner, gathering edges evenly as you work, until entire edge is securely stapled. Trim fabric even with lower edge of board (Figure 3).

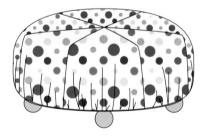

Figure 3

3. Serge short edges of center ruffle strip with right sides together. Finish one long edge with overlock stitch. Sew a gathering stitch along opposite edge and pull threads to gather to a 2-inch diameter opening. Glue gathered edge of ruffle to top of tuffet with opening surrounding the center.

4. Follow manufacturer's instructions to cover 3-inch covered button form with scrap of contrasting pin dot

fabric. Cut two long pieces of waxed button thread. Using the two lengths as one, slide the button shank onto the center of the thread.

5. Insert upholstery needle eye-side up through the hole in the board and out through the center of the fabric-covered top.

Note: *If needed, cut a small hole for needle in the fabric.*

6. Insert all ends of the thread through the eye of the needle. Pull thread through the foam and the hole in the board. Remove needle. Insert thread ends through holes of two-hole button and pull tightly to indent the center of the tuffet with the button. Knot threads securely, tying several knots.

7. Glue one length of chenille ball fringe around bottom edge of tuffet. Glue second length of ball fringe over first, allowing top edge of first layer to show and alternating position of pompoms with first layer. §

Sources: Fabric from Michael Miller Fabrics; Nu-Foam upholstery foam alternative from Fairfield Processing; chenille ball fringe from Expo International; Dritz Home upholstery needle, waxed button thread, cover button form and staple gun and staples from Prym Consumer USA Inc.; Americana acrylic paint from DecoArt; Fabri-Tac permanent fabric adhesive from Beacon Adhesives.

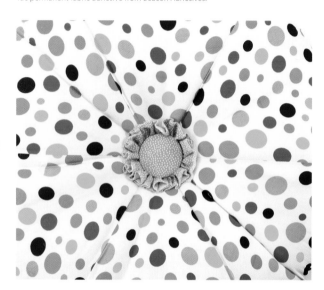

More Than a Gift

Sewing is a special way to show how much you care. Spend a few minutes to serge these fast gifts for friends and family.

Tote Trio Use your serger to make this tote and accessories in an afternoon. This is a great gift, but take time to serge a trio for yourself too!

By Carol Zentgraf

Tote

Finished size

12 x 15 x 6 inches, excluding straps

Materials

• 44-inch-wide cotton fabric:
    1 yard reversible quilted
    ⅝ yard coordinating print
• 4 x 5-inch scrap second coordinating print
• 1¼-inch square cover button form
• Double-stick fusible web tape:
    ¼ inch wide
    ½ inch wide
• 3 or 4 cones serger thread
• Basic sewing supplies and equipment

Cutting

From reversible quilted fabric:

• Cut six 4½ x 19½-inch rectangles for tote upper bands.
• Cut two 7½ x 19½-inch rectangles for tote lower bands.
• Cut two 4 x 28-inch strips for straps.

From coordinating print fabric:

• Cut two 19½ x 19½-inch squares for lining front and back.

From scrap of second coordinating print fabric:

• Cut one 1 x 5-inch strip for button loop.
• Cut one 3 x 3-inch square for button cover.

Assembly

Use a 3- or 4-thread overlock with a ¼-inch-wide seam allowance and medium stitch length, unless otherwise stated. Sew right sides together. Press as you sew.

1. Serge together long edges of three upper bands and one lower band, alternating prints, for tote front (Figure 1). Repeat to make tote back.

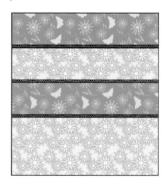

Figure 1

2. Serge tote front and back together, matching seams, along side and bottom edges. To box bottom, align side and bottom seam line at each corner and pin. Draw a stitching line 3¼ inches from each point. Stitch on lines. Trim seam allowances.

3. Serge side and bottom edges of lining front and back, leaving a 6-inch opening for turning in one side. Box bottom as for tote.

4. Apply ½-inch-wide fusible web tape along both long edges on the wrong side of each strap. Remove paper backing, turn under edges and press hems in place. Press each strap in half lengthwise, wrong sides together. Edgestitch all side edges.

5. Use ¼-inch-wide fusible web tape to hem long edges of button loop in same manner. Fold in half lengthwise with wrong sides together and edgestitch.

6. Pin ends of one strap to top edge of tote front, 5 inches from each side seam, with ends extending ½ inch beyond top edge of tote. Repeat on tote back with second strap. Fold button loop in half and pin ends to center of top edge of tote back (Figure 2).

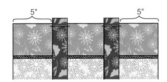

Figure 2

7. Place tote inside lining with right sides together, side seams matching and upper edges aligned. Sew upper edges together, stitching twice for reinforcement.

8. Pull tote through opening in lining, turning lining right side out. Sew opening closed and insert lining in tote. Press top edge and topstitch.

9. Follow manufacturer's instructions to cover button with fabric. Sew button to center of tote front top edge.

Cosmetic Bag

Finished size
5½ x 6½ x 1 inches

Materials
• Scraps cotton print fabric:
    8½ x 7½-inch rectangle print
    8½ x 7½-inch rectangle coordinating print
      for lining
    3 x 3-inch square same coordinating print
      for button cover

• 2 (8½ x 7½-inch) rectangles low loft batting
• 5 inches ½-inch-wide hook-and-loop tape
• 1¼-inch square cover button form
• 3 or 4 cones of serger thread
• Basic sewing supplies and equipment

Assembly
Use a 3- or 4-thread overlock with a ¼-inch-wide seam and medium stitch length unless otherwise stated. Sew right sides together. Press as you sew.

1. Serge a batting rectangle to the wrong side of each rectangle print. Serge rectangles together along side and bottom edges.

2. Serge lining rectangles together along side and bottom edges, leaving a 2-inch opening for turning in center of bottom edge.

3. Box bottom of bag and lining as for tote (step 2), measuring 1¼ inches from points to mark stitching lines.

4. With right sides together and seams aligned, place bag inside lining. Serge upper edges together. Pull bag through lining opening, turning lining right side out. Tuck lining inside bag and press.

5. Sew hook-and-loop strips inside bag ¾ inch from upper edges. Fold upper edges to outside above tape strips. Topstitch close to folded edge.

6. Follow manufacturer's instructions to cover button. Sew button to front of bag.

Eyeglass Case

Finished size
6¼ x 2½ inches (for readers), or 6¼ x 3 inches (for larger glasses)

Materials
• Scraps cotton print fabric:
>   7 x 7-inch square print
>   7 x 7-inch square coordinating print
>   2 x 24-inch bias strip cut from same
>   coordinating print for binding
• 2 (7 x 7-inch) squares low loft batting
• 1-inch bias tape maker
• 3 or 4 cones of serger thread
• Basic sewing supplies and equipment

Cutting

From 7 x 7-inch square print:
• Use template to cut one eyeglass case on fold.

From 7 x 7-inch square coordinating print:
• Use template to cut one eyeglass case on fold.

From 7 x 7-inch square lowloft batting:
• Use template to cut one eyeglass case on fold.

Assembly
Use a 3- or 4-thread overlock with a ¼-inch-wide seam and medium stitch length unless otherwise stated.

1. Sandwich batting between wrong sides of fabric eyeglass case pieces, matching edges. Serge edges together.

2. If desired, lightly quilt layered fabrics with rows of machine stitching.

3. Follow manufacturer's instructions to make binding from bias strip using bias tape maker. Wrap binding over edges of layered fabrics. Straight-stitch close to inside edge.

4. Fold case in half with edges even; pin. Referring to pattern, begin at the X and straight-stitch edges together along side and bottom edge to fold. **§**

Sources: Fabric from Fabri-Quilt Inc.; Poly-Fil low-loft batting from Fairfield Processing Corp.; cover buttons from Prym Consumer USA; Steam-A-Seam 2 fusible web tape from The Warm Company; bias tape maker from Clover Needlecraft Inc.

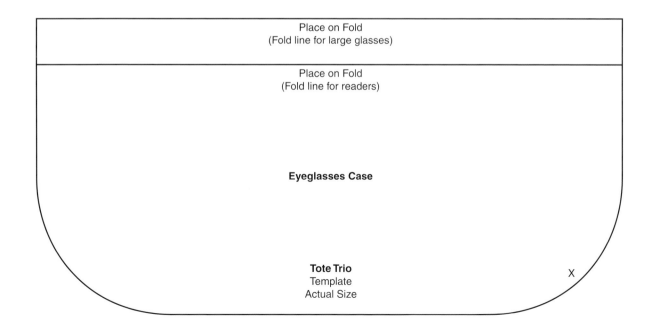

Place on Fold
(Fold line for large glasses)

Place on Fold
(Fold line for readers)

Eyeglasses Case

Tote Trio
Template
Actual Size

X

Rolled-Around Tree Skirt

Add the finishing holiday touch to a tabletop-tree display with this serger-savvy tree skirt.

By Donelle McAdams for Sew Biz

Finished size

27 inches in diameter

Materials

- 44/45-inch-wide lightweight woven fabric:
    - ⅞ yard holiday print for skirt
    - ⅓ yard coordinating print for ruffle
- 1½ yards ⅜-inch-wide ribbon
- 1 cone of woolly nylon or decorative thread for rolled edge
- 3 or 4 cones serger thread
- Basic sewing supplies and equipment

Tips & Techniques

- *When doing rolled edge, allow serger to sliver-cut approximately ⅛ inch of fabric.*

- *Sew hem in skirt edges with wrong side up, stitching through center of overlock stitches and using edge of presser foot as a guide.*

- *To gather, use a gathering foot and straight stitch. Increase top tension 25 percent and set stitch length to 4.5 or 5 (basting stitch length). Test on a 12-inch-long piece of scrap fabric. It should gather to 6 inches. Adjust length and tension as needed.*

Cutting

From holiday print fabric:

- Cut one 15-inch strip the width of the fabric for skirt piece (A).
- Cut two 15 x 21-inch strips for skirt pieces (B).

From coordinating print fabric:

- Cut four 2½-inch strips the width of the fabric for ruffle.

Assembly

Use 3- or 4-thread overlock with ¼-inch-wide seam and medium stitch length, unless otherwise stated. Use polyester or poly/cotton blend thread. Refer to your owner's manual for rolled edge set up. For a decorative effect use woolly nylon thread in the upper looper if desired. Sample project uses poly/cotton thread in the upper looper. Press as you sew.

1. Using rolled edge as a seam, serge short ends of four ruffle pieces with right sides together. Leave thread tails.

2. With fabric facing right side up, roll-edge finish the two short ends of ruffle. Leave thread tails.

3. With fabric still right side up, finish both long edges of ruffle with rolled edge. ***Note:*** *This will cut off thread tails of seams and ends.* Leave thread tails at beginning and end of long edges. Apply seam sealant to thread tails at the four corners. Let dry before cutting tails. Set ruffle aside.

4. Set serger for 3- or 4-thread overlock. With right sides together, serge one 15-inch edge of each skirt (B) piece to 15-inch edges of skirt (A) piece. Press seams toward (B) pieces.

5. With right side up, serge all four sides of skirt. Use double-ended eyelet tool or chenille needle to thread serger tails back into overcast stitch.

6. Press under short edges of skirt 1 inch. Using regular sewing machine, straight stitch close to finished edge to form hem.

7. On one long edge of skirt, press under 2¼ inches to form casing. Straight stitch 1 inch from folded edge. Stitch again 2 inches from folded edge (Figure 1).

Figure 1

Full-size Skirting

This tree skirt can be made to fit a full-size tree using the same technique.

• Purchase 5 yards of fabric. Cut a 5- to 7-inch-wide strip off both long sides and sew together for ruffle.

• Finish edges of ruffle and skirt as for treetop skirt. Gather ruffle 1½ inches from one long edge and fold down 4 inches on skirt for casing; stitch at 2½ and 3¾ inches from fold.

• Cut 2 yards of ribbon in half and securely stitch one end of each length to ends of 27-inch length ¾-inch-wide elastic. Thread through casing.

8. Stitching ⅝ inch from one long edge (this will be the top edge), gather ruffle to half its length.

9. Divide and mark ruffle and lower edge of skirt each into eight sections. Place upper edge of ruffle right side up on lower edge of skirt so gathering line of stitching is ⅜ inch above finished edge of skirt. Pin ruffle in place, matching sections (Figure 2).

Figure 2

10. Using sewing machine set for straight stitch, sew directly on top of gathering stitches.

11. Thread ribbon through top casing and tie ends to gather skirt. Remove ribbon to launder. §

Woven Candle Mat Use brightly woven
strips of coordinating fabrics to create a unique base for a
display of candles or flowers.

By Lorine Mason

Finished size

16 x 16 inches

Materials

• 44/45-inch lightweight woven fabric:

  ¼ yard print (A)

  ¼ yard print (B)

  ¼ yard print (C)

  ¼ yard print (D)

• 3 or 4 cones serger thread

• Basic sewing supplies and equipment

Cutting

From print (A) fabric:

• Cut two 2-inch strips the width of the fabric
  for weaving strips.

From print (B) fabric:

• Cut two 2-inch strips the width of the fabric
  for weaving strips.

From print (C) fabric:

• Cut two 2-inch strips the width of the fabric
  for weaving strips.

• Cut two 2-inch strips the width of the fabric for binding.

From print (D) fabric:

• Cut four 2-inch strips the width of the fabric
  for border.

Assembly

Use a 3- or 4-thread overlock with a ¼-inch-wide seam
and medium stitch length, unless otherwise stated.
Use polyester or poly/cotton blend thread. For a
decorative effect, try using pearl cotton or baby yarn
in the upper and lower loopers. Press as you sew.

1. With wrong sides together, serge long edges of one
A and one B strip together. Repeat with second A and
B strips. Trim each serged strip into 14-inch lengths.

2. With wrong sides together, serge long edges of two C strips together. Trim into 14-inch lengths.

3. Lay the strip even with a set of vertical lines on the cutting mat. Lay a second strip horizontally across the top corner of the first strip. Pin the corner. Lay a third strip horizontally under the edge of the vertical strip, aligning it with the lines on the cutting mat. Repeat to the bottom of the vertical strip.

4. Weave additional vertical strips between the horizontal strips, alternating prints and using the three C strips in the center. Pin strips as you place them.

5. Sandwich edges of mat between two border strips and serge raw edges together (Figure 1). Trim border strips even with mat. Repeat on opposite side of mat, then on top and bottom.

6. Serge ends of binding strips together using a diagonal seam. Press seam open. Press strip in half lengthwise with wrong sides together. Open fold and press raw edges to center crease, then refold and press.

7. Open binding strip. Turn beginning end under. Pin binding to borders, matching raw edges and mitering corners. Serge binding to mat.

8. Fold binding over border raw edges and hand-stitch to bottom side of mat or stitch-in-the ditch to finish. §

Figure 1

Tips & Techniques

Use blue painter's tape to attach strips to cutting mat and to hold strips together at each overlap. Place tape in center of strip for easy removal after serging on borders.

Serge Organize A simple serged chateline for around her neck and a sewing caddy for under her machine make great gifts for your sewing friends.

By Barbara Rezac

Finished sizes

Chatelaine: 53 inches long with 1¼-inch-wide neck ribbon
Caddy: 18 x 18 inches

Materials

• 44/45-inch lightweight woven fabric:
  - ¾ yard for background
  - ½ yard for pocket
• ⅝ yard 44/45-inch-wide mediumweight woven fabric for backing
• 1⅜ yards coordinating piping
• 6 x 8 inches paper-backed fusible web
• 5-inch fusible tape
• Threads:
  - 2 spools 12-weight multicolored cotton thread
  - 4 cones serger thread
• Optional: glue stick
• Piping foot
• Basic sewing supplies and equipment

Cutting

From background fabric:

• Cut one 21 x 24-inch rectangle for caddy front.
• Cut one 2½ strip the width of the fabric for neck ribbon.

From pocket fabric:

• Cut one 21 x 10-inch rectangle for back pocket.
• Cut one 21 x 15-inch rectangle for front pocket.

• Cut one 7 x 3½-inch rectangle for pin cushion.
• Cut two 6 x 8-inch rectangles for scissors holder.

From backing fabric:

• Cut one 21 x 19-inch rectangle for backing.

From piping:

• Cut two 21-inch lengths.

Caddy Assembly

Use a 3- or 4-thread overlock with ¼-inch-wide seam and medium stitch length. Sew right sides together. Press as you sew.

1. Attach piping foot to serger. Position a length of piping across each long edge of back pocket rectangle (Figure 1). **Note:** *A glue stick may help hold piping in place.*

Figure 1

2. Serge 21-inch edge of caddy front to one piping edge of back pocket. Serge one long edge of front pocket to the opposite piping edge of back pocket. Press fabric to expose piping.

3. Accordion-fold pockets so the two piped edges are approximately 1¾ inches apart (Figure 2). **Note:** *The bottom fold of the back pocket is above the bottom edge of the front pocket.* Press bottom fold in back pocket. Pin fold in place.

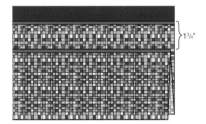

Figure 2

4. Fold caddy front so fold is even with raw edge of front pocket (Figure 3). Press fold in fabric.

Figure 3

5. Pin backing to caddy background and pocket unit with right sides together. Serge one edge. Fold serged seam under, folding right on the needle thread to create a wrapped corner, then stitch the second side. Repeat on each edge, leaving an opening on one side for turning.

6. Turn caddy right side out. Press. Close opening with a ¼-inch-wide strip of fusible tape.

7. Mark pocket divisions at 4½-inch intervals from side and stitch using sewing machine.

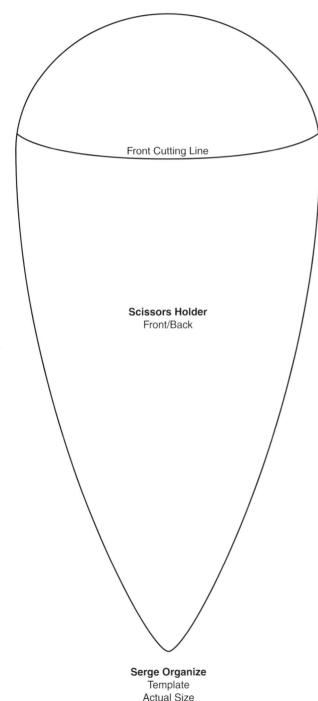

Front Cutting Line

Scissors Holder
Front/Back

Serge Organize
Template
Actual Size

Chatelaine Assembly

Leave serger set for 4-thread overlock. Thread both loopers with 12-weight multicolored cotton thread.

1. Fold neck ribbon in half lengthwise with wrong sides together. Serge four sides.

2. Fold pincushion piece in half to make a 3½ x 3½-inch square. Serge around one folded edge and two additional sides. Stuff with fiberfill, then serge fourth edge closed.

3. Place the fabric for the scissor holder front and back pieces with wrong sides together. Following manufacturer's instructions, fuse the pieces together using paper-backed fusible web. Using scissors holder template, cut one front and one back. Serge across the upper curved edge of front piece.

4. Place front and back together, aligning edges. Serge outer edges.

5. Use sewing machine to stitch one end of neck ribbon to pincushion and opposite end to scissors holder. §

Sources: Steam-A-Seam 2 fusible web from The Warm Company; Blendables multicolored cotton thread from Sulky of America.

Cupcake Apron
Cupcakes are the new birthday cake, so why not serge up a fun cupcake apron to gift for the special occasion!

By Lorine Mason

Finished size
Adult medium/large

Materials
• 44/45-inch lightweight woven fabric:
     1½ yard cupcake print
     1 yard coordinating solid
• 3 or 4 cones serger thread
• Basic sewing supplies and equipment

Cutting
Enlarge templates for apron front/back and pocket front/lining as indicated.

From cupcake print fabric:
• Cut one apron on fold.
• Cut one pocket.
• Cut four 4-inch strips the width of the fabric for pleated ruffle.
• Cut three 3-inch strips the width of the fabric for binding.

From coordinating solid fabric:
• Cut one apron lining on fold.
• Cut one pocket lining.

Assembly
Use a 3- or 4-thread overlock with a ¼-inch-wide seam and medium stitch length unless otherwise stated. Press as you sew.

1. Serge short ends of 3-inch binding strips together using diagonal seams. Press binding strip in half lengthwise with wrong sides together. Open strip and press raw edges toward center fold; press. Fold again on center fold and press. Set aside.

2. Serge short ends of 4-inch pleated ruffle strips together using diagonal seams. Press ruffle strip in half with wrong sides together, matching long edges. Mark strip in 1-inch increments across. Pin and fold 2-inch box pleats in ruffle, with the first pleat measuring 2 inches from the end (Figure 1). Machine-baste raw edge of pleated ruffle. Set aside.

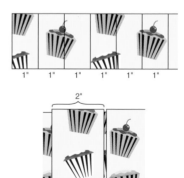

Figure 1

3. Pin apron and apron lining with right sides together, matching raw edges. Serge across top edge. Turn right sides out, letting lining extend ¼ inch above

top of apron front. Pin apron sections together with wrong sides together. Press.

4. Pin pleated ruffle around edges of apron front and lining with raw edges even; trim excess ruffle. Serge ruffle to apron. Press ruffle away from apron and seam toward lining.

5. Pin remaining section of ruffle to top edge of pocket front, centering pleats. Trim ruffle, leaving ½ inch at each end. Turn ends to inside.

6. With right sides together, pin pocket and pocket lining together. Serge around edges, leaving a 4-inch opening on one side. Turn right side out. Press.

7. Pin pocket on apron 16 inches from top and topstitch ¼ inch from side and bottom edges.

8. Cut a 122-inch length of 3-inch binding made in step 1. Mark center of binding with a pin. Beginning

11 inches from marked center on each side, pin binding to upper sides of apron, encasing raw edges and folding raw ends of binding to inside (Figure 2). Topstitch binding in place, catching edges on both sides of apron and continuing stitching to complete ties and neck strap. **§**

Figure 2

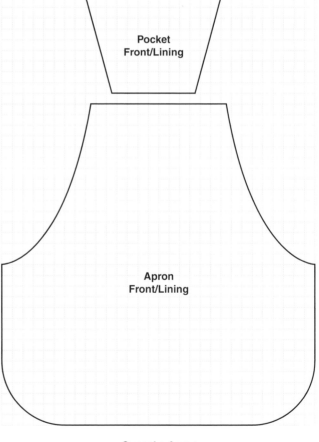

Cupcake Apron
Templates
1 square = 1"

Sweet Tote Whether you are a room mother or a baker on the go, this handy carrier is an easy way to get your confections to their destination in style!

By Linda Turner Griepentrog

Finished size

Fits a 9 x 14 x 4-inch cake/cupcake carrier

Materials

• 44/45-inch-wide lightweight cotton fabric:

    1 yard cupcake print

    1 yard coordinating print for lining

• 2 (16-inch-long) ½-inch acrylic rods

• ¼ yard ⅝-inch-wide hook-and-loop tape

• Double-fold bias tape to match

• 3 or 4 cones serger thread

• Basic sewing supplies and equipment

Cutting

Press each fabric thoroughly to remove folds. Spray wrong side of one fabric with temporary adhesive. Layer fabrics wrong sides together and smooth into place. Enlarge outer wrap and inner wrap templates (page 154) as indicated.

From bonded cupcake and coordinating prints:

• Cut one outer wrap.

• Cut one inner wrap.

Assembly

Use a 3- or 4-thread overlock with ⅛-inch-wide seam and a short stitch length. Use polyester or poly/cotton blend thread. For a heavier, firmer edge, use texturized nylon or polyester thread in both loopers. Press as you sew.

1. Serge perimeter (omitting handle openings) of both outer wrap and inner wrap.

2. Bind edges of handle openings with double-fold bias tape (Figure 1).

Figure 1

3. Wrap inner wrap lengthwise around cupcake holder and pin-mark the overlap. Center hook-and-loop tapes across the wrap width on each end and stitch in place (Figure 2).

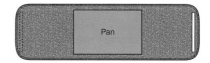

Figure 2

Tips & Techniques

To make an insulated casserole cover, insert fusible batting between fabric layers. Baste all layers together along cut edges before serging. Or use double-face quilted fabric, narrowly zigzagging cut edges to prevent separation.

4. Center the inner wrap over the outer wrap in both directions. Pin layers in place and straight stitch 1 inch inside the overlap ends and along the serging on the sides (Figure 3).

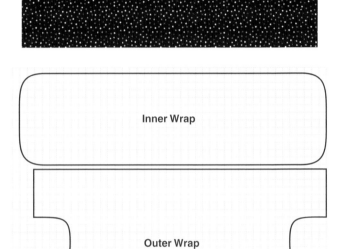

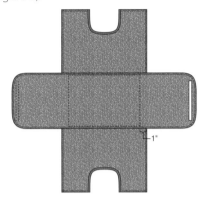

Figure 3

Figure 4

5. Fold the handle casing 1¾ inches toward lining side and straight stitch the edges and outer ends in place. Slip ends of acrylic rods into handle casings (Figure 4). §

Source: Thread from Sulky of America.

Inner Wrap

Outer Wrap

Sweet Tote
Templates
1 square = 1"

Flatlock Patchwork Tote

Join the patchwork pieces with decorative flatlock to create your own colorful patchwork fabric for a fun-to-serge gift.

By Marta Alto

Finished size
9½ x 11½ x 4½ inches

Materials
• ⅛ yard each of at least 7 different fabrics in desired color scheme; mix solids with prints
• ⅝ yard 44/45-inch-wide cotton broadcloth for lining
• ⅝ yard 44-inch-wide lightweight fusible knit or weft-insertion interfacing
• ½ yard polyester fleece
• 1 yard paper-backed fusible web
• ¼ yard nonwoven suede for the straps
• 1⅝ yards 1-inch-wide non-roll waistband interfacing
• 6½ yards ¼-inch-wide paper-backed, self-adhesive fusible web tape
• Threads:
    1 ball No. 8 pearl cotton for serging in color to match or contrast with tote fabrics
    1 spool of buttonhole twist for flatlock
    3 or 4 spools serger
• 4 (1- or 1½-inch) decorative buttons with shanks
• Buttonhole twist
• Basic sewing tools and equipment

Cutting
From each of seven different fabrics:
• Cut seven or eight 3¼-inch squares for a total of 50 squares for tote patchwork and a few for stitch testing.

From lining fabric:
Refer to Lining Cutting Layout on page 158.
• Cut two 15 x 15-inch squares for lining front and back.
• Cut one 10 x 18-inch rectangle for large pocket.
• Cut one 4 x 8-inch rectangle for cell phone pocket.
• Cut one 4½ x 11-inch rectangle for glasses pocket.

From lightweight fusible interfacing:
• Cut two 15 x 15-inch squares for lining front and back.
• Cut one 10 x 18-inch rectangle for large pocket.
• Cut one 4 x 8-inch rectangle for cell phone pocket.
• Cut one 4½ x 11-inch rectangle for glasses pocket.

From polyester fleece:
• Cut two 15 x 15-inch squares for front and back.

From paper-backed fusible web:
• Cut two 15 x 15-inch squares for front and back.

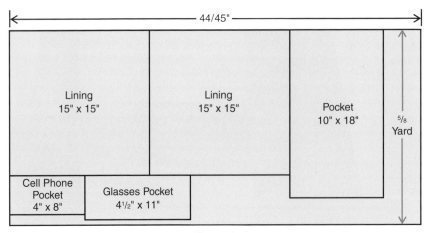

Figure 1
Lining Cutting Layout

From nonwoven suede:
• Cut two 2½ x 28-inch strips for straps.

From the waistband interfacing:
• Cut two strips each 27¾ inches long for straps.

From self-adhesive fusible tape:
• Cut four 28-inch lengths.

Assembly
Use a 3- or 4-thread overlock with ¼-inch-wide seam and medium stitch length, unless otherwise stated. Use polyester or poly/cotton blend thread. Refer to your owner's manual for flatlock setup. When flatlocking, shorten the stitch length and set the width at the widest setting. Use pearl cotton in the upper looper for a decorative effect

Note: Serging with heavier thread, like pearl cotton, requires slower stitching and special tension and length settings. Test stitches on extra tote patchwork squares before assembling tote.

1. Arrange tote patchwork squares in five rows of five squares each for tote front. Repeat for tote back. Number each row with a small scrap of paper.

2. Working one row at a time, pin squares with wrong sides together and raw edges even. Serge squares together in each row, barely trimming seam allowance (Figure 2). Pull open and flatten seams in each row (Figure 3).

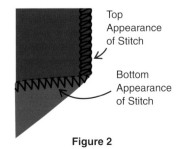

Top Appearance of Stitch

Bottom Appearance of Stitch

Figure 2

Figure 3

3. Pin and serge rows together, matching seams. Flatten and press seams to create patchwork front and back.

4. Apply each front/back square of fusible web to one side of each front/back square of fleece following the manufacturer's directions. Remove the backing paper on each fusible-backed fleece square. Fuse a fleece square to the wrong side of each patchwork piece.

5. With right sides together, use sewing machine to straight stitch tote front and back together on sides and bottom, using ¼-inch seam allowance.

6. Align side and bottom seam lines at each corner and pin in place. Draw a stitching line 2¼ inches from the point and stitch on the line to box bottom of tote (Figure 4). Turn the bag right side out and finger-press the corner seams as needed.

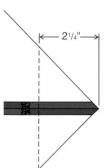

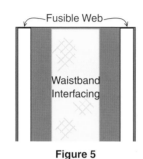

Figure 4   **Figure 5**

7. On wrong side of each suede strap piece, center two lengths of ¼-inch paper-backed fusible tape side by side. Fuse in place and remove paper backing. Center a piece of waistband interfacing over fusible web tape. Using press cloth, fuse in place. Apply another length of fusible web tape to each long raw edge on the wrong side of each strip (Figure 5).

8. For each strap, wrap one edge of the strap over the interfacing and fuse in place. Repeat with the remaining long edge to encase the interfacing. Topstitch ¼ inch and ⅜ inch from each long edge.

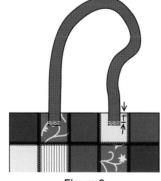

9. Referring to Figure 6, position straps on bag front and back, and stitch in place three or four times close to the raw ends.

Figure 6

10. Following the manufacturer's directions, fuse interfacing pieces to wrong sides of corresponding lining pieces. Fold interfaced pockets in half with right sides together and straight stitch edges using a ¼-inch seam allowance and leaving an opening

in each one for turning (Figure 7). Clip corners and turn right side out. **Note:** *Pivoting and stitching at the opening as shown in the illustration makes it easier to turn the raw edges in to finish the pocket neatly.*

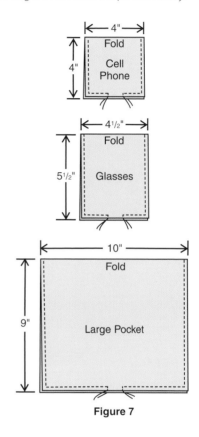

Figure 7

continued on page 174

Tips & Techniques

If desired, substitute a serged and overlapped seam for the flatlocked seams by serging one edge of each square, then overlapping squares and machine-stitching in place.

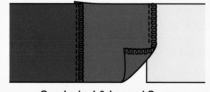

Overlocked & Lapped Seam Alternative

Serger Bag Trio Use holiday fabrics and decorative serger techniques to present the perfect gifts in the perfect bags!

By Pamela Hastings

Bottle Bag

Finished size

14 x 5 x 2½ inches

Materials

• 44/45-inch-wide woven fabric:
  ⅜ yard holiday print for bag
  ½ yard coordinating print for cuff
• Threads:
  Cotton to match or contrast
  Pearl cotton or heavy embroidery
    flatlock embellishment
  3 or 4 cones serger
• 28 inches ⅜-inch-wide ribbon
• Basic sewing supplies and equipment

Cutting

From holiday print fabric:
• Cut one 16 x 9½-inch rectangle for bag.

From coordinating print fabric:
• Cut one 16 x 12-inch fabric for cuff.

Assembly

Use 3- or 4-thread overlock with ¼-inch-wide seam and medium stitch length, unless otherwise stated. Use polyester or poly/cotton blend thread. For a decorative effect for the flatlock, use pearl cotton or baby yarn in upper looper. Refer to your owner's manual for flatlock setting. Press as you sew.

1. Fold fabric in half with right sides together, matching short edges, and serge across sides (Figure 1). Press seam.

Figure 1

2. With right sides together, refold the bag, centering seam on one side. Serge along bottom edge of bag (Figure 2). Press seam.

Figure 2

3. To box the bottom of the bag, flatten the bottom seam so side seam matches the bottom seam and a point is formed. Pin fabric. On each side, serge a 2½-inch-long line across the bottom of the bag 1¼ inches from point tip.

4. Fold cuff in half with right sides together, matching the short edges. Serge across raw edges. Press seam.

5. Refold cuff with wrong sides together. Pin cuff inside bag, matching seams and raw edges. Refer to owner's manual for flatlock setting. Thread pearl cotton or embroidery thread in upper looper. Flatlock cuff to body (Figure 3). Pull cuff up to flatten the stitches. Press.

Figure 3

6. Fold ribbon in half and finger press to mark center. Pin center of the ribbon over back seam 4 inches from top of cuff. Straight stitch ribbon in place on seam line (Figure 4). Tie ribbon in a bow around cuff to close.

Figure 4

Gift Bag

Finished size
14 x 10½ x 4 inches

Materials
• 44/45-inch-wide woven fabric:
    ½ yard bright print fabric for bag
    ¼ yard coordinating print fabric for cuff
• 20 inches ⅞-inch-wide grosgrain ribbon
• Basic sewing supplies and equipment

Cutting
From bright print fabric:
• Cut one 13½ x 30-inch rectangle for bag.

From coordinating print fabric:
• Cut one 6 x 30-inch rectangle for cuff.

Assembly
Use 3- or 4-thread overlock with ¼-inch-wide seam and medium stitch length, unless otherwise stated. Use polyester or poly/cotton blend thread. Press as you sew.

1. Fold bag rectangle in half with right sides together, matching short edges. Fold the ribbon in half and finger press. Sandwich ribbon between short edges of fabric ½ inch from top edge with ribbon fold even with raw edges of fabric (Figure 5). Serge seam catching ribbon as you serge.

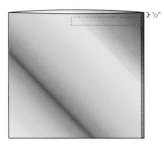

Figure 5

2. Follow steps 2–4 for Bottle Bag above, serging a 4-inch-long line across bottom of bag 2⅛ inches from each point.

3. Pin cuff to gift bag with right sides together and raw edges even, matching seams. Serge edges together, keeping ribbon free of seam. Press seam toward bag. Tie ribbon in a bow around cuff to close.

CD Bag

Finished size
8 x 10 inches, unfolded

Materials
• 44/45-inch-wide woven fabric:
    ¼ yard holiday print for bag
    ¼ yard coordinating print for cuff

• 24 inches ⅞-inch-wide grosgrain ribbon
• Basic sewing supplies and equipment

Cutting
From holiday print fabric:
• Cut two 8 x 7-inch rectangles for bag.

From coordinating print fabric:
• Cut two 8 x 7-inch rectangles for cuff.

Assembly
Use 3- or 4-thread overlock with ¼-inch-wide seam and medium stitch length, unless otherwise stated. Use polyester or poly/cotton blend thread. Press as you sew.

1. Pin bag rectangles right sides together with raw edges even. Fold ribbon in half and finger press. Sandwich ribbon between layers of fabric in center of one 8-inch (bottom) edge with ribbon fold even with raw edges of fabric. Serge side and bottom edges, catching ribbon (Figure 6). Turn right sides out.

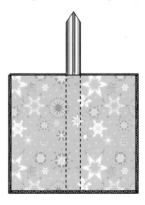

Figure 6

2. Place cuff rectangles right sides together with raw edges even. Serge across two short (side) edges. Fold cuff in half with wrong sides together matching raw edges and seams.

3. With right sides together and matching raw edges, pin cuff to bag. Serge edges together using a 3-thread overlock. Fold cuff up.

4. Insert CD in bag and fold top of bag down. Tie ribbon in a bow around bag to close. §

Sources: Fabric from Michael Miller Fabrics and Freespirit.

Beach Bag Coated cotton fabric makes this roomy tote perfect for carrying to the beach!

By Pamela Hastings

Finished size

13 x 15 x 8 inches

Materials

- 44/45-inch-wide cotton fabric:
    - 1¼ yards colorful print
    - 1⅝ yards coated coordinating print
- ⅛ yard mediumweight interfacing
- 12½ x 7½ inches heavyweight interfacing for bottom insert
- 3 or 4 cones serger thread
- Basic sewing supplies and equipment

Cutting

Enlarge lower bag template (page 170) as indicated.

From colorful print cotton fabric:

- Cut two 23 x 15-inch rectangles for upper bag front and back.
- Cut four 1½ x 24-inch strips for handles.

From coated coordinating print cotton fabric:

- Use template to cut two lower bags on fold.
- Cut two 23 x 15-inch rectangles for upper bag lining front and back.
- Cut two 12½ x 7½-inch rectangles for bottom insert.

From mediumweight interfacing:

- Cut two 2½ x 24-inch strips for handles.

Assembly

Use a 3- or 4-thread overlock with ¼-inch-wide seam width and medium stitch length unless otherwise stated. Use polyester or poly/cotton thread. Use a cool iron to press to avoid melting plastic coated fabric.

1. Fold each lower bag piece in half with right sides together, matching side seams on each end. Serge side seams (Figure 1). Press on cotton side of fabric.

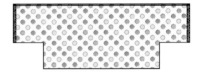

Figure 1

2. Refold each lower bag piece, centering side seams and matching short raw edges. Serge across raw edges on each end to form boxed bottom (Figure 2).

Figure 2

3. Fit one lower bag piece inside the other with wrong sides together. Baste together around top edge. **Note:** *Coated side of lower bag is the outside.*

4. Pin upper bag front and back with right sides together. Serge across short edges (Figure 3). Press seams. Repeat with upper bag lining front and back pieces.

Figure 3

5. Place upper bag lining inside upper bag with wrong sides together and raw edges even. Serge top raw edges even. Baste bottom raw edges together.

6. Turn top ½ inch to outside of bag. Topstitch in place along serged edge.

7. With outside of lower bag facing outside of upper bag, pin basted edges even. Machine stitch using a ½-inch seam allowance, then serge along seam to finish edge.

8. Press seam toward bottom of bag. Topstitch on outside of bag ⅛ inch from seam.

9. Fold interfacing strips for handles in half lengthwise to measure 2¼ inches wide each. Layer one folded interfacing strip between wrong sides of two fabric handle strips. Serge around all four edges of each handle unit.

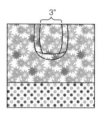

Figure 4

10. Center handles on each side of bag, spacing ends 3 inches apart (Figure 4). Topstitch each end in place. §

Source: Fabric from Michael Miller Fabrics.

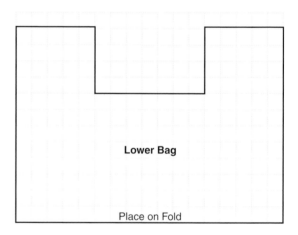

Beach Bag
Template
1 square = 1"

Jelly Roll Shopping Tote

Precut jelly roll packs offer color coordinates perfect for this foldable shopping tote. A serger rolled hem accents the pieced seams with aplomb.

By Linda Turner Griepentrog

Finished size

16½ x 15 x 3½ inches

Materials

- ⅞ yard 60-inch-wide cotton duck fabric
- Jelly roll pack with at least 14 (2½-inch-wide) strips
- Paper-backed fusible web
- Set 23-inch rolled-leather handles
- 3 cones serger thread
- Basic sewing supplies and equipment

Cutting

Enlarge Tote Lining template (page 172) as indicated.

From cotton duck fabric:

- Use template to cut one tote lining on double fold.
- Cut one 27 x 24-inch rectangle for tote bottom.
- Cut one 2 x 12-inch strip for handle attachments.

Assembly

Use a 3-thread overlock with a narrow seam width and a short stitch length unless otherwise stated. Use polyester or poly/cotton blend thread. For a decorative effect, try using pearl cotton or baby yarn in upper looper with a narrow 3-thread overlock.

1. Serge long edges of 11 jelly roll strips with wrong sides together. Lightly press all strip seams in one direction.

2. Lay wrong side of pieced strips over tote lining and pin in place, aligning tote lining edge with edge of a jelly roll strip. Baste ⅛ inch from lining edges (Figure 1). Trim strip section to match tote lining.

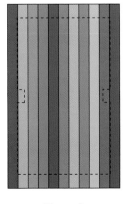

Figure 1

3. Turn both short edges of tote bottom rectangle to middle and press folded edges. Fuse raw edges in place with strips of fusible web.

4. With pieced strips facing up, center folded tote bottom over corner squares at bottom area of tote (Figure 2). Fuse folded edges in place.

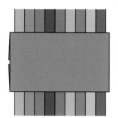 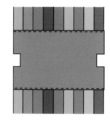

| **Figure 2** | **Figure 3** |

5. Topstitch folded edges of tote bottom through all layers. Cut out corner squares on tote bottom to match tote lining/strip section (Figure 3). ***Note:*** *Strip section is right side of tote.*

6. Fold tote right sides together with edges even and matching upper edges of bag bottom. Serge side seams (Figure 4). Using an extra jelly roll strip, bind raw edges of side seams.

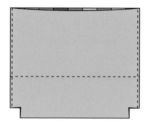

Figure 4

7. Fold bottom of bag, matching edges of corner cutouts. Stitch across corners (Figure 5). ***Note:*** *This is a very heavy seam. A larger needle may be needed.* Bind raw edges as for side seams, or serge to finish.

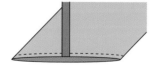

Figure 5

8. Fold long edges of handle attachment strip to center of strip. Fuse in place. Topstitch folded edges. Cut strip into four 2¾-inch-long pieces. Slip each piece through handle loops with fused edges inside. Baste ends together.

9. Mark the upper tote center front and back. Stitch each loop to the tote 4 inches from the center on the wrong side, being careful not to twist the handles (Figure 6).

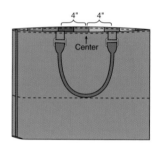

Figure 6

10. Using an additional jelly roll strip, bind the bag upper edge. Fold the handles up and stitch across the binding upper edge to hold them upright. §

Sources: Bali Pop-Sherbet jelly roll from Hoffman California Fabrics; Steam-A-Seam 2 paper-backed fusible web from The Warm Company; Jitney rolled leather handles from Peacock Patterns.

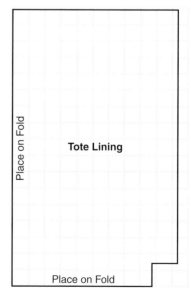

Jelly Roll Shopping Tote
Template
1 square = 1"

Starry Night Tote Use your serger's cover stitch for perfect topstitching and the chain stitch for a simple decorative finish.

By Nancy Estep

Finished size

15 x 9½ x 2 inches, excluding handles

Materials

• ½ yard tan duck or canvas fabric
• ½ yard navy blue star-print mediumweight
   cotton fabric
• 1 yard batting
• 1 yard ¼-inch piping cord
• ½-inch bias tape maker
• 1½-inch button
• ½-inch-wide paper-backed self-adhesive fusible web
• Threads:
      12-weight cotton to match cotton fabric
         for chain stitch
      3 or 4 cones serger
• Basic sewing supplies and equipment

Cutting

From tan duck or canvas fabric:

• Cut one 16 x 19-inch rectangle for tote.
• Cut one 2 x 36-inch strip for handles.
• Cut one 1¼ x 36-inch bias strip for piping.

From navy blue star-print mediumweight cotton fabric:

• Cut one 16 x 19-inch rectangle for tote.
• Cut two 5 x 12½-inch rectangles for outer pockets.
• Cut one 16 x 6-inch rectangle for lining pocket.
• Cut one 31½ x 3½-inch strip for top trim.

• Cut 1-inch bias strips: two 20-inches; one 36 inches for trim on handles; one 10-inches for tab closure. Use bias tape maker to fold and press, following manufacturer's instructions.

From batting:

• Cut one 15½ x 18½-inch rectangle for tote.
• Cut one 31½ x 1½-inch strip for top trim.

Assembly

Use a 3- or 4-thread overlock with ¼-inch-wide seam and medium stitch length, unless otherwise stated. Use polyester or poly/cotton blend thread. Press as you sew.

1. Draw a line on right side of tote rectangle 2½ inches from right side, parallel with 19-inch measurement. Draw a second line 5 inches to the left of the first line. Between parallel lines, lightly mark 2½ inches from top and bottom edges of tote for pocket placement (Figure 1).

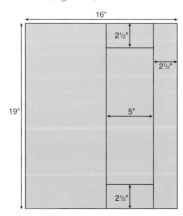

Figure 1

2. Set serger to a chain stitch. Using 12-weight cotton thread, sew decorative stitches horizontally across the spaces above the pocket placement lines and vertically in the area to the left of the pocket placement (Figure 2).

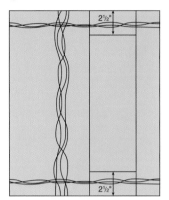

Figure 2

3. Secure batting to wrong side of tote rectangle with temporary spray adhesive, leaving ¼ inch of fabric extending around batting.

4. Fold each outer pocket rectangle in half, right sides together, to form a 5 x 6¼-inch rectangle. Serge the raw edge opposite the fold, leaving sides unfinished. Turn to the right side and press. Press the folded edge down 1 inch.

5. Position pockets between placement lines, making sure top (folded) edges of pockets are toward ends of tote (Figure 3). Topstitch across bottom of each pocket close to edge.

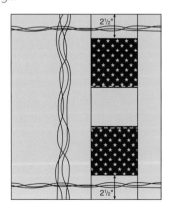

Figure 3

6. Set serger to a wide cover stitch. Place one of the 20-inch folded bias strips over one of the parallel lines, covering the raw edges of both pockets. Sew in place using cover stitch on serger. Repeat on opposite side of pockets with remaining 20-inch folded bias strip (Figure 4).

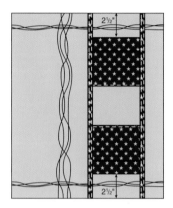

Figure 4

7. Press long edges of handle strip to center and hold in place with ½-inch-wide self-adhesive fusible web. Press to fuse. With serger still set to a wide cover stitch, sew 36-inch folded bias strip over raw edges of handle strip. Cut handle in half. Set aside.

8. Serge stripe with cover stitch. Set aside.

9. Reset serger to 4-thread overlock. Serge sides of tote (Figure 5). Press bottom fold.

Figure 5   **Figure 6**

10. Flatten bottom of tote, matching pressed fold with side seams. Stitch across point at each end to box bottom of tote (Figure 6).

11. Attach piping foot on serger. Wrap 36-inch bias strip for piping over piping cord. Serge raw edges of strip to cover cord. Serge covered piping cord to top of bag, beginning and ending at one side seam.

12. Spray temporary adhesive on wrong side of top trim fabric strip. Place top trim batting ¼ inch away from one raw edge and press in place. ***Note:*** *Batting will cover only half the strip.* With right sides together, serge short ends of strip together; turn.

13. Adjust serger for chain stitch. Fold trim strip in half with wrong sides together. Using chain stitch and 12-weight cotton thread, stitch decorative stitches across strip to hold batting in place.

14. Reset serger for 4-thread overlock. With right sides together, serge raw edge of top trim to top edge of tote using piping foot (Figure 7).

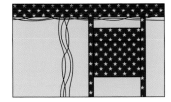

Figure 7

15. Mark center front and back of tote. Place a handle 3 inches on each side of center mark on front and back (Figure 8). Baste in place. Form a loop from 10-inch bias strip and baste ends at center back between handles for closure loop.

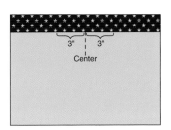

Figure 8

16. With wrong sides together, fold raw edge of fabric on long side of lining pocket ¾-inch. Fold fabric once again, this time matching right side to right side. Serge through three fabric layers to create a ¾-inch hem on one long edge of lining pocket. Press under ¼ inch on opposite edge. Place pocket right side up on right side of lining, 1½ inches from top matching side edges (Figure 9). Topstitch across bottom edge of pocket. Stitch through pocket to divide into three equal sections.

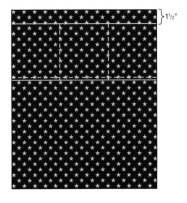

Figure 9

17. With right sides together, serge sides of lining, leaving an opening for turning on one side. Box bottom of lining as for tote (step 10).

18. With right sides together, place lining inside tote. Serge around top. Turn tote right side out through opening in lining. Machine- or hand-stitch opening closed. Arrange lining inside tote.

19. Sew button on tote front to correspond with closure loop. §

Source: Steam-A-Seam 2 paper-backed fusible web from The Warm Company.

Flatlock Patchwork Tote

Continued from page 159

11. Position pockets on lining front and back and topstitch in place (Figure 8). With right sides facing, sew the lining pieces together along the side and bottom edges; leave a 6-inch-long opening in the bottom. Do not turn the lining right side out. Box the bottom corners as described for the tote.

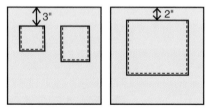

Figure 8

12. Following package directions, apply the magnetic snaps 1 inch below the upper edge of the lining so they will be centered under the straps on the patchwork on completed tote.

13. With right sides facing, tuck tote into lining. With upper raw edges even, straight stitch layers together ¼ inch from the edge. **Note:** *Use a ¼-inch foot (or a zipper foot), if necessary, to stitch past the snaps.*

14. Turn tote right side out through opening in lining. Turn under seam allowances in lining opening and edgestitch together. Tuck lining into tote.

15. Topstitch or edgestitch the lining and tote together around the upper edge, catching the straps in the stitching. Position the shank of a decorative button at the lower raw edge of each strap end and sew in place with buttonhole twist. §

Special Thanks
Please join us in thanking the talented designers listed below for sharing their serger designs with us.

Marta Alto
Flatlock Patchwork Tote, 156

Brenda Bornyasz
Serge Simple Shirt, 76

Janis Bullis
Quick Cuddly Quilt, 34
Trim a Tee, 61

Laura Dollar
Bow Tie for Baby, 41
Summer Breeze, 24

Nancy Estep
Elegant Embroidered Runner, 125
Pintuck Shirt, 64
Starry Night Tote, 170

Zoe Graul
Tailored for Me Oxford, 72

Sue Green-Baker
Heirloom Pillow, 128
Picture-Perfect Place Setting, 114
Quick & Easy Pillow Cover, 111

Linda Turner Griepentrog
Jelly Roll Shopping Tote, 167
Sweet Tote, 153

Marianne Guy
All-Stitched-Up Denim, 54
Jeweled Batik Jacket, 98

Pamela Hastings
Baby Steps, 38
Beach Bag, 164
Jelly Roll Valance, 108
Serger Bag Trio, 160

Dorothy Martin
Cozy Cover, 44

Lorine Mason
Cupcake Apron, 150
Funsie Onesie, 21
Smart Serged Sweatshirt, 49
Woven Candle Mat, 143
Yo-yo Baby Quilt, 27

Donelle McAdams
Rolled-Around Tree Skirt, 140

Barbara Rezac
Flatlock Fleece, 86
Scrappy Braid Place Mat, 122
Serge Organize, 146
Princess P.J.s, 79

Suzy Seed
Puzzle Blouse, 69
Rectangle to Jacket, 66

Cheryl Stranges
Coverstitch: More Than Hems, 90
Serge a Simple Jacket, 94

Carolyn Vagts
Reversible Batik Topper, 118

Lynn Weglarz
Fast & Breezy Skirt, 84
Heirloom Baby Bib, 30
Rolled Around Tee, 58

Carol Zentgraf
Button Valance, 102
Fly-Away Drapery, 105
Polka Dot Tuffet, 131
Tote Trio, 136

Sewing Sources

The following companies provided fabric and/or supplies for projects in this book. If you are unable to locate a product locally, contact the manufacturers listed below for the closest retail or mail-order source.

Beacon Adhesives Inc.
(914) 699-3405
www.beaconcreates.com

Brensan Studios
www.brensan.com

Clover Needlecraft Inc.
(800) 233-1703
www.clover-usa.com

DecoArt
(800) 367-3047
www.decoart.com

Expo International
(800) 542-4367
www.expointl.com

Fabri-Quilt Inc.
(816) 421-2000
www.fabri-quilt.com

Fairfield Processing
(800) 980-8000
www.poly-fil.com

FreeSpirit Fabric
(866) 907-3305
www.freespiritfabric.com

Hoffman California Fabrics
(800) 547-0100
www.hoffmanfabrics.com

Husqvarna Viking Sewing
Machine Co.
(800) 358-0001
www.husqvarnaviking.com

Jennifer Amor
(803) 256-0146
www.jenniferamor.com

June Tailor
(800) 844-5400
www.junetailor.com

Kwik Sew Pattern Co. Inc.
(888) 594-5739
www.kwiksew.com

Michael Miller Fabrics
(212) 704-0774
www.michaelmiller
fabrics.com

Peacock Patterns
(414) 416-8205
www.peacockpatterns.com

Prym Consumer USA Inc.
www.prymdritz.com

Shannon Fabrics Inc.
(866) 624-5252
www.shannonfabrics.com

Sulky of America
(800) 874-4115
www.sulky.com

The Warm Company
(425) 248-2424
www.warmcompany.com

Westminster Fibers
www.westminsterfibers.com

YLI Corp.
(803) 985-3100
www.ylicorp.com

Basic Sewing Supplies & Equipment

- Sewing machine and matching thread
- Serger
- Scissors of various sizes
- Rotary cutter(s), mats and straightedges
- Pattern tracing paper or cloth
- Pressing tools such as sleeve rolls and pressing boards
- Pressing equipment, including ironing board and iron; press cloths
- Straight pins
- Measuring tools
- Marking pens (either air- or water-soluble) or tailor's chalk

- Spray adhesive (temporary)
- Hand-sewing needles and thimble
- Point turners